MW00462987

# MEDITATIONS at SIXTY

## One Person, Under God, Indivisible

Kashrut, Modesty, Mourning, Prayer and Love

# MEDITATIONS at SIXTY
## One Person, Under God, Indivisible

Kashrut, Modesty, Mourning, Prayer and Love

Eliyahu Safran

Ktav Publishing House, Inc.

Copyright©2008
Eliyahu Safran

Library of Congress Cataloging-in-Publication Data


Safran, Eliyahu.
  Meditations at sixty : kashrut, modesty, mourning, prayer and love /
Eliyahu Safran.
     p. cm.
  ISBN 978-1-60280-038-0
  1. Jewish way of life. 2. Spiritual life–Judaism. 3. Jews–Dietary
laws. 4. Modesty–Religious aspects–Judaism. 5. Jewish mourning customs.
6. Love–Religious aspects–Judaism. 7. Jewish ethics. 8. Miracles. I.
Title.
  BM723.S238 2008
  296.7–dc22
                                                    2008020637


Published by
KTAV Publishing House, Inc.
930 Newark Avenue
Jersey City, NJ  07306
Email:  bernie@ktav.com
www.ktav.com
(201) 963-9524
Fax (201) 963-0102

FOR MY KLARI

רבקה שרה בת ר׳ יהושע ואלטע רחל לאה תחי׳

WITH
LOVE, GRATITUDE AND RESPECT
ELIYAHU

# CONTENTS

# INTRODUCTION

Judaism is unique in its articulation of the relationship between body and soul; the physical and the spiritual. The meditations included in this modest volume explore the depth of that relationship in ways that allow the individual reader to begin to divine greater meaning in his or her life.

Too often, our modern world demands that we choose the physical, or the spiritual. But how do we decide between the two? For Jews, there is authentic holiness in the physical, in the embrace of the world, and physical expression in the spiritual. We see it in every aspect of Jewish ritual behavior.

To those who have not explored the spiritual power of ritual, ritual is often misunderstood as being simply "legalistic;" the rote expression of religious habit. In fact, that criticism is often cast against Judaism in general; that it is a "legalistic" religion rather than a "spiritual" religion.

As I hope to make clear in my meditations, nothing could be further from the truth.

The 613 Torah mitzvot represent specific ways to engage *every* part of one's body and every part of the world in harmonious, *sacred* action. Nothing in our physical beings is too "base" to be imbued with the sacred. And nothing in our spiritual lives is ever divorced from the body in which our souls are housed.

Many religions and philosophies seem determined to "transcend the world." Such a goal is foreign to Judaism. Judaism's purpose is to recognize the Divine in the world, to lift up the world and, by doing so, perfect oneself.

Judaism is a continual engagement with the world. Mitzvot guide us in the appropriate ways to engage the world, not to avoid the world. For Jews, hunger is not simply a physical drive; it is an opportunity to interact with the divine! *That* is what we need to understand when we examine the meaning of *kashrut*. It is not simply a list of rules but an engagement with that which is most divine.

It is the marriage between our bodies and our souls.

These meditations explore in depth that interface between the physical and the spiritual world and the balance between the two. It is important to engage in this discussion because the demands of our modern world have thrown the two powerfully out of balance. Which is one of the reasons I have engaged in this project now.

In this volume, I discuss the traditional Jewish view of modesty, of *tzniut*. In the modesty meditation, I explore the power of *tzniut* not to hide but to display that which is most beautiful about our lives; I have included essays on *kashrut*, prayer, mourning, honesty, love, and the power of paradox in Jewish tradition. In each of these essays, or meditations, I explore what is essential to them and to the greater ethos of Judaism.

In the essay on *kashrut*, *I* note that hunger is an essential physical drive of all living things. But like all essential drives, unless it is satisfied in a way that is both permissible and holy, it is impossible to enjoy a spiritual life. The essential truth is that there is *no* bodily desire or function that is not rooted in an equally essentially soul desire.

Each of us has before us a choice in everything we do. There is the right way, and the wrong way. We can satisfy our hunger drive as every other animal in creation or we can find the holiness in this physical activity and have it become a mirror of the Divine. After all, we all must eat. Still, from a Jewish perspective the adage, "you are what you eat" is not a comment on good health alone but a comment on your spiritual self and goes to not only what you eat but how you eat, when you eat, where you eat and why you eat.

In my meditation on Honesty, I note that our modern world often asks, What harm is there in a small bit of deception – a *small* lie – if no one gets hurt in the process?

Such a *laissez faire* attitude might carry the day amongst those for whom honesty and dishonesty are not character traits but tolerable – and equally allowable – strategies for getting ahead in the world; to be employed as the situation dictates and used for advantage.

But there is a reason that *"laissez faire"* is a language other than Hebrew. Jewish law is clear in the matter of such ethical dishonesty: engaging in any form of intellectual dishonesty, including cheating on exams, plagiarizing, is strictly forbidden. It is non-negotiable.

My essay on "the service of one's heart" – on prayer – poses important questions and insights. Jewish tradition teaches that prayer is both action and posture, both verb and noun. It bridges and it is the bridge. Prayer is an affirmation of love and faith. When the Torah teaches us *ulevodo bkhol levavkehm*, "loving the Lord your God and serving Him with all your heart and soul," the Talmud asks, "What is service of the heart? What is *avodah shebalev?*"

The simple fact is, nothing in our world is just "as it seems." Such a view might be satisfying to a child but not to one who is willing to wrestle with the greater issues of life. Life is often paradox, as I suggest in another essay. How do we know who we are? What we are? How do we know who we are *supposed* to be?

How do we *know* anything?

Perhaps the observant Jew could provide an adequate answer. He might tell us that we know who we are and who we are supposed to be because God tells us. God tells us we are to be holy because God is holy.

Those of us who seek to be wise as well as observant, who seek understanding as well as knowledge would find such a response dissatisfying.

In these, and the other meditations, there is a much deeper understanding to my topic than might first appear. Whether that has to do with the historical and mystical truths evident in the simple "toy" we spin at Chanukah or the powerful Jewish ethos that demands honesty in business and in personal dealings, the message is clear: Judaism does not consider the physical and spiritual to be at odds. Rather, they are dual expressions of the same brilliance of Creation, the expressions of a loving Creator who expects much from us and who has given us more.

There is, also, a more heartfelt and personal reason for my devoting myself to this volume now. It has everything to do with understanding what is most important in life and what we seek to accomplish in the "blink of an eye" that is our lifetime.

More than twenty years before my father passed away, he drafted his will which said, in part, thank you to G-d "with all my heart and soul for having granted me the privilege to see the publication of my work.... This is an event of inordinate importance in my life, and I am filled with gratitude to Him for helping me after much toil and great efforts to attain this life yearning."

With those words, he then turned to his children and noted his request that they "frequently and insightfully" study and "look into the books" he had written. "You and your dear children..." and then he concluded with "...a great request... that you frequently study in the responsa works of my father, the great Gaon, so that his soul be uplifted , and in this merit he will always beseech Him on your behalf and that of your families."

As a young man, I confess that my father's words did not fully resonate with me but as I advance in years and I too began to meditate on the world after I am gone, I find myself sharing my dear father's sentiments that my children and, please G-d, their children and their children too might be able to share in something real and meaningful that I have left behind.

In the more than seventy years since my grandfather, Rav Bezalel Zev Shafran left this world, his "*She'elot U'tshuvot RBAZ*" continue to be studied and cited by great Talmidei Chachamim, all over the world.   More than a decade after my father, Rabbi Dr. Joseph Safran, left us, his monumental three-volume work "*Pirkei Iyun B'Toldot HaChinuch HaYehudi*" has assumed its rightful place among the most important works concerned with all facets of Jewish education.

Of my grandfather's physical possessions, none remain.  Of my father's physical possessions too, nothing remains.

But their thoughts and ideas...?  These endure.  The ideas, lessons, and messages transmitted from father to son to grandson and to the many generations yet to come continue to live and thrive.

Thus it is that these modest meditations are informed – samplings of lessons, lectures, writings to students of all ages, shared over the past four decades in New York, New Jersey, Pennsylvania and elsewhere... Please God, one day my grandchildren will teach the very same lessons and, quite naturally, improve upon them...

And if one day, someone will ask my children and grandchildren, What did your grand father Eliyahu do in this world? I will be blessed if they are able to reply that I left some Torah thought and teachings.

These meditations and others.

And so, I dedicate them to my children and grandchildren. I pray that God in His kindness grant for Klari and me many more healthy, peaceful, productive, meaningful and spiritual years together with all of our beloved children and grandchildren.

Nisan 5768 – May 2008

# CALLED TO BE DIFFERENT; CALLED TO BE HOLY

## A MEDITATION ON KASHRUT

All that lives upon the earth must breathe. All that lives upon the earth must drink. All that lives upon the earth must eat.

All that lives upon this earth is a physical being and, as such, is driven by fundamental needs that enable each living thing to survive. Human beings – people – share these drives with every beast of the field or fowl of the air; with each creature that crawls in the dust or which soars through the vault of blue sky.

*Thus the heavens and the earth were finished, and all the host of them. And on the seventh day God ended His work which He had made; and He rested on the seventh day from all His work which He had made. And God blessed the seventh day, and sanctified it; because that in it He had rested from all his work which God created and made.*

*These are the generations of the heavens and of the earth when they were created, in the day that the Lord God made the earth and the heavens. And every plant of the field before it was in the earth, and every herb of the field before it grew; for the Lord God had not caused it to rain upon the earth, and there was not a man to till the ground. And a mist went up from the earth, and watered the whole face of the ground. And the Lord God formed* Adam *of the dust of the ground* (adamah), *and breathed into his nostrils the breath of life; and* Adam *became a living soul.*

In *Breishit*, the Torah makes clear that the "stuff" from which we were formed (adamah) is integral and essential to who and what we are (Adam.) In other words, the physical world matters. What's more, we were formed from the very same "stuff" as even the most base creature in God's creation. Our physical form and nature was taken from the "dust of the ground." We are physical beings.

Buddhism, like many Eastern religions and philosophies, seeks meaning by seeking to turn away from the physicality of life, of somehow "escaping" the ever-turning wheel of birth and death. According to Buddhism, salvation – nirvana – is the transcendent reality of escaping this endless cycle. But Judaism, unlike Buddhism and the other religions and philosophies that share its necessarily nihilistic perspective, does not seek to deny our physical nature. To do so would be to deny something essential and important, indeed something spiritual, about who we are. As Jews, we are taught to embrace the physical. To do anything less would be to question the wisdom and sanctity of God's creation.

"I have set before you life and death, therefore choose life."

Life.

Life is good. Creation is good. The physical world is good.

However, while we *share* physicality with every living thing in creation, we are not *the same* as every living thing. Far from it. We are not simply the physical form that we inhabit.

"And the Lord God formed Adam of the dust of the ground and breathed into his nostrils the breath of life; and Adam became *a living soul.*"

Like every other creature in creation, our physical needs demand fulfillment if we are to survive, to remain in this "mortal coil." But, distinct from every other creature in creation, we received something *more* than just our physical selves. We received the "breath of life" from God. We received a soul.

A body *and* a soul.

BODY AND SOUL –

For the Jew, there is holiness in the physical, in the embrace of the world. In fact, there is a profound misunderstanding by non-Jews and nonobservant Jews when it comes to the *mitzvot* that define a Jewish life. Often, there will be the criticism that Judaism is a "legalistic" religion rather than a "spiritual" religion. Nothing could be further from the truth.

The 613 Torah mitzvot represent a specific way to engage *every* part of one's body and every part of the world in harmonious, *sacred* action. Nothing in our physical beings is too "base" to be imbued with the sacred. For example, not long ago I was conversing with a nonobservant Jew who was particularly enamored by Eastern religion in a public place when a gentleman, a religious Jew, came out of the washroom. He paused for a moment, turned his face to the wall and, with his eyes closed, he mouthed something silently.

"What's he doing?" my nonobservant friend asked.

"He's saying a blessing."

"A blessing?" he asked in astonishment. "For what?"

I smiled. "Just as there is a blessing before and after eating or drinking, there is likewise a blessing to say after using the toilet," I explained. I could see that my explanation was leaving my friend even more confused.

"Blessings," I went on, "put us in touch with the sacred nature of what we do. The blessing that gentleman just said acknowledges the Divine as the source of all bodily functions." Sanctifying the most basic of physical activities gives one the potential to rise to the level of the Divine throne.

So many religions seek to transcend the world. Judaism's purpose is to lift up the world and, by doing so, perfect oneself.

That seemed somewhat revelatory to my friend. That the sacred might be found in something as *purely physical* as using the toilet completely astonished him. I pointed out to him that the Kabbalah teaches that every physical object possesses some sparks of holiness.

"When we use an object in the way in which it was intended – our bodies included – we release the sparks and they can reunite with the Divine. You see, our role here in this world is to lift the whole of creation…"

My friend shook his head in wonder. The proponents of the Eastern religions he had explored had uniformly tried to separate the spiritual from the physical and yet here, in its most elemental sense, was Judaism's celebration of the Divine in every single aspect of our physical beings.

Judaism's focus is holiness and spirituality, no less than it is the focus of my friend's Eastern religions. However, the physical is never abandoned. It is embraced as a full partner on the path to holiness.

The divergence of perspective between Judaism and Eastern religions is most pronounced when we speak of any of the primal "drives" that animate our physical beings. Certainly, the way in which Judaism embraces sexuality is significantly different than most Eastern – and many Western – religions and philosophies. Whereas many Eastern religions place celibacy – denial – at the pinnacle of the human expression of this drive, Judaism describes the union between a married couple as the "holy of holies." Certainly Judaism *regulates* sexual behavior. The Torah *obligates* a man to sexually satisfy his wife.

How different this is from other "religious" approaches to sexuality!

Isn't this embrace of the physical and the spiritual together the underlying message of the laws of the Sabbath? For six days, we are commanded to work, to dirty our hands, to fully engage the world; but on the seventh day, we are commanded to put aside our labors, to "rest". By "rest" we are not meant to lay on a couch but to *actively* engage ourselves in our spirituality. Tradition teaches us that we receive an additional soul of the Sabbath, and with it, the ability to glimpse the full holiness of the Divine.

Religions and philosophies that seek to deny or denigrate the physical must, by definition, deny that life itself has a purpose (other than to deny that it has a purpose!) Rabbi Aryeh Kaplan, in the *Handbook of Jewish Thought*, wrote, "The foundation of Judaism and the basis of all true religion is the realization that existence is purposeful, and that man has a purpose in life. Both man and nature have meaning because they were created by a purposeful Being."

Man has a purpose *in life*. Not *in spite of* life, but *because* of it.

The question then is, What is the purpose of life?

Sounds like a question that one of those devotees of Eastern religion would utter, doesn't it? But, in a surprise to my nonobservant friend, it is *the* essential question of Judaism.

"But, *that's* why I began to explore Buddhism to begin with," he protested. "I wanted to answer that question. I wanted to understand the meaning of life…"

While individual Jews are often motivated to seek purpose and spirituality in life, they sadly rarely look to their own Jewishness as a source of that purpose and spirituality. These individuals then struggle with a philosophy that teaches that the purpose of life is to "attain enlightenment" which, too often, means turning away from the world in the name of "spiritual consciousness." Judaism teaches that the purpose of life is not spiritual consciousness alone but that holiness and spirituality is the result of refined action (mitzvot). Whereas Eastern religions hold that enlightenment can be attained through meditation, Judaism teaches that life's purpose requires not only prayerfulness (meditation) but also the performance of mitzvot, consecrated *actions*.

A physical act performed without some spiritual consciousness, what would be termed *kavanah* in Hebrew, is simply that, a physical act. For it is only with *kavanah*, the consciousness that the act is the will of God with the purpose of coming closer to God, that the physical act is made sacred.

This is why "mitzvah" is so often defined as a "good deed." Mitzvot are positive behaviors. They are *good* things. But good is not necessarily holy. To be holy, the act must carry with it a *consciousness* of holiness, a sense of the Divine.

A human being is body *and* soul together. The soul, being a small spark of God's sacred flame, does not require attention. It is already perfect. However, in order to experience the sacred in this world, we need to perfect the physical, that which is *not* yet perfect, in order to live a holy life.

Torah commandments are physical because through the fulfillment of those mitzvot each of us can train our bodies so that they might be sanctified as well. It is in the sanctification of the physical that we realize the sanctity of our hearts and minds as well.

"Love your neighbor as yourself."

Who could criticize with such a command? It is at the foundation of community. But, *how* do you love your neighbor as yourself? Not by *feelings* but by behaviors which demonstrate respect in clear, measurable ways, by how we treat our neighbor with respect and dignity.

Why? Because it is *in* the world that we find meaning and order.

"God caused every kind of tree to grow from the ground, attractive to the sight and good for food..." (Breishit 2:9)

Why would the verse mention that the trees were "attractive to the sight" before "good for food"? Our rabbis suggest that this shows that both aspects are important – beauty and taste – and that failing to appreciate both in a permissible way goes against God's plan in creating the trees.

"Be fruitful and multiply."

Jews are commanded to marry, raise families, live in a home, earn a living. We are commanded to be fathers and mothers, to engage in the world, not remove ourselves from it.

Judaism is a continual engagement with the world. Mitzvot guide us in the appropriate ways to engage the world, not to avoid the world. Which brings us to *kashrut*.

Hunger is an essential drive of all living things. But like all essential drives, unless it is satisfied in a way that is both permissible and holy, you can not enjoy a spiritual life. The essential truth is that there is *no* bodily desire or function that is not rooted in an equally essentially soul desire.

Each of us has before us a choice in everything we do. There is the right way, and the wrong way. We can satisfy our hunger drive as every other animal in creation or we can find the holiness in this physical activity and have it become a mirror of the Divine. After all, we all must eat. Still, from a Jewish perspective the adage, "you are what you eat" is not a comment on good health alone but a comment on your spiritual self and goes to not only what you eat but how you eat, when you eat, where you eat and why you eat.

There are those – good intentioned, intelligent and knowledgeable – who hold that the laws of *kashrut* were established primarily as a guide to healthy living. "Trichinosis" is often the first word out of their mouths when a discussion of dietary laws and habits is engaged.

Unfortunately, such a perspective completely misses the essence of the laws of *kashrut*. What's more, the argument logically leads to the conclusion that kosher laws are outdated. After all, the trichinosis and exotic food borne diseases that existed in the desert certainly no longer exist in the modern age of refrigeration. When was the last time that someone in a Western country became sick with trichinosis?

The attempt to give a "logical" rationale for keeping kosher is misguided. The command to observe *kashrut*, like every other *mitzva* is significant and spiritual not because of the content of the command but because it is God who has commanded it. As Maimonides wrote, "It is appropriate that one meditate, according to his intellectual capacity, regarding the laws of the Torah to understand their deeper meaning. Those laws for which he finds no reason and knows no purpose should nevertheless not be treated lightly."

What is Maimonides saying here? Ultimately, we follow the commandments not because they "make sense" or even because they have an intrinsic logic. We follow the commandments as an article of faith. To do otherwise would turn our relationship with God upside down. Do we follow a commandment because it makes sense to us? Of course not. That would suggest that the following of the commandment was dependent on our deeming it satisfactory. That is clearly not the case.

*Mitzvot* require no explanation. The Mishnah states (Brachot 5:3) that, "One who [in referring to the *mitzvah* of chasing away of the mother bird before taking her eggs or chicks] says, 'even young birds merit your kindness,' is silenced."

When we seek to understand a *mitzvah* we should not concern ourselves so much with what is accomplished with the *mitzvah* as much as what lessons we can draw from it. Does any of us really believe that God requires us to care for His creatures? He has many ways at His disposal to care for them. What then might be the purpose of this *mitzvah*? Maimonides teaches that the purpose of chasing away the mother before taking her eggs or chicks is so that we can internalize feelings of compassion.

The "reason" behind the *mitzvah* is hidden from us. We should seek to understand what we can understand from it. At the very least, performing a *mitzvah* elevates its performance from being just a physical act to an act that brings us closer to God.

So, with this understanding, let us finally dismiss the notion that *kashrut* is about physical health. The Torah is not merely a medical textbook! *Kashrut* is about spiritual health! Like other *mitzvoth*, it is not for the body but for the soul.

In order to understand just how important *kashrut* is to the Jewish soul, we should first examine what it is that distinguishes one person, or group of persons, from another. It is fairly easy to identify a member of a professional sports team. He or she wears a distinctive uniform that identifies him or her. However, even that is not a sufficient marker. Professional jerseys and uniforms are available for purchase in thousands of different places. Just wearing a uniform is not enough to make a person a member of the team.

To be a member of a team, and to be correctly identified with that team, an individual must engage in the behaviors and practices of that team. It is not enough to "look the look and talk the talk" you must also "walk the walk." *Kashrut* is a fundamental way of keeping Jews spiritually sensitive to *being Jewish*. In other words, walking the walk.

So, our rabbis have suggested, the purpose of *kashrut* is to keep us separate from others, to keep us from assimilating. Certainly there is wisdom in this understanding. *Not* eating what my neighbor eats distinguishes me from him and keeps me from assimilating.

If my non-Jewish neighbor, whom I like and think is a very decent person, invites me to join him for a MacDonald's cheeseburger or even for a meal at his house, I have to say, no. *Kashrut* defines physical-spiritual boundaries that define who I am, and who I am not. As a result of these boundaries, I eat with fellow Jews, socialize with fellow Jews, shop with fellow Jews. In short, my social context is my religious context.

If all Jews kept *kashrut* there is no doubt that our rate of intermarriage would drop significantly. Why? Because when Jews socialize with other Jews, it is more likely that they will find "Jewishness" attractive and so be attracted to a Jewish mate.

This "attractiveness" is more than simple physical attraction. In a more significant way, keeping kosher does much more than simply "limit" our food choices or our choices in dining partners. It keeps us attracted to our Jewishness, to our spirituality, to all things Jewish.

It transforms the simple act of eating into an affirmation of who we are, and who we are intended to be.

For the Jew, non-kosher foods are bad for the health. But not physical health. Spiritual health.

You really *are* what you eat.

*Mitzvot* establish the parameters of a Jewish life. They define what we can and can't do if we are to live Jewishly. Our *mitzvot* distinguish us from everyone else. And, in doing so, they define what it means for us to be holy.

While it is true that everyone eats – criminals, cannibals, animals – a Jew must eat *differently* if he is to elevate this essential physical act into an expression of spiritual longing. By their very nature and existence, the laws of *kashrut* teach us compassion and restraint. Before we eat, we wash our hands *and say a blessing* so that we might demonstrate our worthiness to eat even a piece of bread. If three or more sit down to eat together then that meal must not be only about sustenance. We are commanded that when three or more people sit down to eat, words of Torah must pass between them. Our meal must be about more than mere physical food, it must also be about communal holiness.

According to the Torah, if three people enjoy a feast and words of Torah are not exchanged then it is as if they had partaken of a dead offering – prohibited and repulsive. It is the spiritual that gives life to the food, not the other way around.

Jews recite blessings both before and after eating, connecting body to soul. By doing so, an essentially physical act becomes a spiritual endeavor, one that reminds us that we are in the presence of an external God. Blessings imbue physical experiences with spiritual significance.

Our rabbis taught that it is forbidden for man to enjoy anything of this world without a blessing. By doing so, he commits a sacrilege.

Blessings are invitations. They invite us to embrace the spiritual while engaging in the physical. They allow us to be both in the world and to be spiritual beings at the same time.

Seeing the spiritual in the physical is the essence of what distinguishes a righteous man from a wicked man. According to the rabbis:

*The wicked man is regarded as dead while living because he sees the sun shining and does not say the blessing "Creator of light," sees it setting and does not say "who brings in the evening twilight," eats and drinks and does not say a blessing. The righteous, however, say a blessing over everything they eat or drink or see or hear.*

To one who is spiritually deaf, dumb and blind, who has "eyes but cannot see, ears but cannot hear, a mouth but cannot speak," there is a wide chasm between the physical and the spiritual. For they cannot utter a blessing, the bridge between the two.

If blessings form the interface between the physical and the spiritual, it seems fair to ask, What exactly are blessings? Blessings begin with the words, "*Baruch atah Hashem…*" These words, almost invariably translated, "Blessed are you, Hashem…" actually pose a more interesting challenge. After all, why would God be in need of being blessed by man?

What does it mean for man to "bless" God?

If "blessing" means to share or bestow something upon another then it clearly makes no sense for man to bless God. However, if to bless means to recognize and understand, then blessing has a more profound significance that *is* relevant to man.

When Jacob "blessed" his sons, he did not simply "wish them well." He spoke to the inherent quality and ability of each. And to each he gave in appropriate measure. In making a blessing, we are closer to Jacob in that we are recognizing an inherent quality in God. That is, God is the One who "brings forth bread from the earth," or "creates the fruit of the trees."

Blessings reinforce our understanding and our recognition of God's majesty and power.

What is magnificent is that we can recognize God's majesty and power in even our most basic physical functions and drives *because* it is God who has imbued that physicality with spirit.

In *Breishit* God declares:

*Be fruitful and multiply, and replenish the earth, and subdue it… And God said, Behold, I have given you every herb yielding seed, which is upon the face of all the earth, and every tree, in which is the fruit of a tree yielding seed – to you it shall be for food.*

God, who created Adam from the adamah, the dust of the earth, created him with the need to eat. However, from the beginning, God placed limits on what Adam could eat. He could eat all forms of vegetation but he could not eat meat. Ramban explained this restriction as indicative of God's original intent regarding the relationship between man and animal. In Eden, the animal was to serve and assist Adam, not become dinner.

The restriction on eating meat was not the only restriction guiding Adam in the Garden.

*And the Lord God took the man, and put him into the garden of Eden to cultivate it and to keep it. And the Lord God commanded the man, saying, Of every tree of the garden you may freely eat; But of the tree of the knowledge of good and evil, you shall not eat of it; for in the day that you eat of it you shall surely die.*

The relationship, the tension and the promise, between the physical and the spiritual that exists in each of us is captured in these verses. God has bestowed upon Adam all of creation. Adam is the perfect natural being, living in the animal kingdom but also transcendent. Restrictions, *mitzvot,* guide him in negotiating the tension and promise of his unique nature.

Adam lives in the material world. Indeed, he is formed from its very substance. He is a physical being. Yet, God has also breathed a soul into him. He is a spiritual being as well.

Physical and spiritual.

Even in Eden, man's experience was defined by this dual nature. *Mitzvot* allowed him to balance the two.

L'HAVDIL –

Of course, we know that Adam fell. How? By eating forbidden food. Certainly, there was nothing intrinsically wrong with eating an apple (presuming that it was, in fact, an apple, that Adam ate.) His health did not fail because of his choice. So, here we see – from the very beginning – that health issues are not elemental to the eating of forbidden food.

No, the reason that Adam fell was because he did what was forbidden by God. In doing so, he removed himself from that which is holy. He ate because he was hungry. Or because the food seemed attractive and tasty. Or simply because his "dining partner" – Eve – wanted him to. In other words, he ate of the fruit of the forbidden tree for all the same reasons that many people eat.

They are hungry.

The food appears appetizing.

Someone suggests that they "try it, you'll like it."

To our modern, secular ears, anyone who would choose *not* to eat something that looked and smelled appetizing, that someone they cared about invited them to taste, would be crazy. The idea of forbidden foods is so contrary to our society, which invites us to try anything and everything – so long as we have the money to pay for it. We live in a culture that cries out, "Try it, you'll like it."

While such an invitation might sound appealing, it actually cuts across the grain of who we are as living beings and, particularly, as Jews. Rather than embracing anything and everything, we are defined by the limits that we place on our behaviors. Who we are is determined by what we choose *not* to do.

We are a discriminating being and how we divide between what we do and do not do is fundamental to who we are. In regards to what we eat, Jews are instructed in the Torah the importance of such discrimination:

*For I am the Lord that brings you out of the land of Egypt, to be your God; you shall therefore be holy, for I am holy. This is the Torah of the beasts, and of the bird, and of every living creature that moves in the waters, and of every creature that creeps upon the earth; To differentiate (l'havdil) between the unclean and the clean, and between the beast that may be eaten and the beast that may not be eaten.*

As Jews, we are taught to discriminate, to differentiate, between that which God has taught us is clean and that which is unclean, between that which can be eaten and that which cannot be eaten, between the pure and the impure. We do not make these distinctions in order to necessarily be "healthier" (although our spiritual health is certainly much improved by keeping God's commands.) We do not make these distinctions in order to suggest that we are "better" than our neighbors, or to limit our interactions with them. We do not make these distinctions for any reason that is necessarily rational or thought-out. We make these distinctions because God has told us to. We make these distinctions because the ultimate goal of everything we do as Jews is "to be holy." And why are we told to be holy? Because God Himself is holy and our goal and our joy and our meaning comes from our ability to begin to approach the degree of holiness that God desires from us.

Indeed, only a short time later in Torah from the above section, it is written: *You shall therefore differentiate between clean beasts and unclean, and between unclean birds and clean; and you shall not make your souls abominable by beast, or by bird, or by any manner of living thing that creeps on the ground, which I have separated from you as unclean. And you shall be holy to me; for I the Lord am holy, and have separated you from other people, that you should be mine.*

As Jews, we are commanded to make distinctions, to be discriminating – in the finer sense of the word – above all that presents itself to us. In other words, we are not to simply, "try it" and "like it." Our judgment is not based on our "liking" something but rather on how successfully it contributes to that spiritual quest of making us holy.

Every aspect of Jewish life is dependent on this sense of separating. Geography – Israel and the nations; time – Shabbat and the holy days and the days of the week; identity – Jew and the nations. It is wholly consistent that God should direct us to distinguish between different foods.

To distinguish, to discriminate, to choose. This ability is reserved for human beings among all the animals in the animal kingdom. Of course, many beasts of the field "choose" but they don't "make choices." I know a man who has a pet dog. He knows that if he places two bowls before his dog, one filled with bread and one filled with chicken and chicken bones, his dog will "choose" the chicken.

But, has the dog made a choice?

From a Jewish perspective, I would say that the answer is, no. The dog has responded to competing drives, both dictated by animal instincts. The kind of choosing that we are called upon to engage in as Jews demands that we engage *more* than our animals instincts, more than our base natures. Indeed, it is this choosing that distinguishes us from the animal kingdom and is the reason that we can aspire to be holy.

To be holy. Ultimately, these three words captures what it means to be Jewish. We are to be holy because our God is holy. Therefore, following His commands, by definition, bring us closer to that goal.

Our culture presents us with a veritable banquet of riches – of sensations and foods, of images and sounds. Why *shouldn't* we partake of everything that is available to us? Why shouldn't we take *advantage* of all that presents itself to us?

The idea that having all the possibilities in the world available to us is an advantage is based on a fundamental understanding of morality as *not* doing something that is wrong. In other words, in our culture to the extent that morality is a consideration it is a consideration cast in the negative. If I am walking along the street and I pass an unoccupied car parked at the curb, its engine running, I am a moral being if I *don't* steal the car and arrive at my destination more quickly.

That is not the Jewish understanding of morality (even though the commandment, "You shall not steal" is decidedly Jewish!) For example, if one is to find himself on a deserted island, one in which there is no other living soul, then one, by definition, cannot steal from anyone else. He cannot kill another. He cannot covet that which belongs to his neighbor for he has no neighbor.

Does that mean that he is living a moral life?

Decidedly not. His "correct living" is a life that is lived correctly by default, without choice and without intention. Without the positive goal, the forward-looking desire, to be holy.

In order to live a life of true morality, of holiness, our lonely friend on his deserted island would have to live amongst others, so that his not stealing and not killing and not coveting represented very real choices that he makes continually.

In other words, we can only be holy by "turning away from" that which is impure, that which is forbidden. It was only the two trees in the Garden of Eden, with the prohibition against eating of their fruit, that enabled Adam to measure himself, that presented him with the potential for holiness. Without those trees and that prohibition, Adam was little more than our friend on his deserted island, doing the "right" thing by default, because there was no "wrong" thing.

God commands us to distinguish (*l'havdil*) between the holy and the profane, between the pure and the impure, between the right and the wrong. We cannot do that without something before us to distinguish! Morality rests with the struggle between turning left and turning right, with choosing the pure over the impure.

My neighbor's dog did not measure his choice. Chicken registered higher in his instincts. He ate that. There was no real distinction. His choice was no more significant than the choice of our friend on his deserted island. There was no choice.

For all the negatives our Western culture is correctly accused of foisting upon us, on this count we must praise it – Western culture has provided us the perfect opportunity to demonstrate our potential to be holy. Of course, it has also made it much, much more difficult to be successful in achieving that potential.

Our society and culture has become frighteningly successful at approximating the moral landscape of that deserted island. Not by the removal of the possibility to do wrong but by the message that one can do *anything* and it is all right.

*Be yourself.*

*If it feels good, do it.*

*If you can't be with the one you love, love the one you're with.*

In our culture of "anything goes" one choice has the same moral weight as another. There is, according to the culture, no pure or impure, no good or bad, just "what is." A recent article in the New York *Times* Sunday magazine section explored a growing field of neural psychology with the perspective that deviations in the brain itself could be used as legal defense for crimes that were committed. In other words, even the moral is reduced to the physical and is, therefore, not really moral.

It is my neighbor's dog choosing between bread and chicken. The dog is "hard-wired" to opt for the chicken. We are "hard-wired" for our behaviors. Therefore, we cannot be, in the strictest sense, culpable. Responsible.

And we cannot be holy.

If everything is good, nothing is bad. If everything is good, there is no choice, certainly no meaningful choice. Therefore, there is no opportunity to distinguish, to discriminate, to be holy.

In these worldview, we are no different from the beasts of the fields because there is no aspect of our existence that is not physical. No spirit. No soul.

No holiness.

Those who argue that people should be free to be and do whatever they want completely miss the point. The world is truly (not artificially, as our current culture proclaims) created in such a way so that aspects of it are wrong. Just because something exists, or is possible, does not make it good.

The reason the world has been created with infinite possibilities is not so we seek to conquer all those possibilities but so that we can conquer *ourselves*. We seek to conquer ourselves *not* because our desire for experience is bad in and of itself but because that which is good about experience is determined by the power of turning away from that which is not to be experienced.

To discriminate. To choose. To be holy.

We are a creature with the potential of remarkable achievement and despicable failure. We are called upon to love and cherish other humans. We are forbidden to murder. We are commanded to discriminate in all manner of behavior that demands our highest consideration.

But why food then? Why should our morality, our holiness, be tied in to choices regarding food?

The answer, insofar as the question of "why" can be adequately addressed when it concerns God's commands, goes back to the creation, when God breathed a soul into Adam. We noted that Adam was formed from the same physical "stuff" as the beasts of the fields; that his name was derived from the Hebrew word for the clay from which his physical nature was formed (*adamah*). It is this fundamental sameness with all things physical which makes *kashrut* so important.

As best we can understand, murder and theft are particularly human flaws. Turning away from such behavior is necessary but it is particularly human.

Hunger is a drive shared by all living things; eating, an activity all creatures engage in.

For this reason, the fundamental *basic-ness* of eating, it is essential that our ability to *l'havdil*, to distinguish and discriminate, engage us in this context. In Judaism, the laws and rules of conduct rarely concern themselves with that which is function of our "higher natures." There does not exist codes of conduct that describe what is necessary for us to do in order to be "great" or to be "wonderful". Instead, we hone in on the more basic, discerning the holiness in even the most basic of behaviors.

Eating, as my neighbor's dog makes clear, is a natural, basic, animalistic process. It is a function entirely of our physical selves. It is a basic drive, necessary for life. There is no "value" naturally attached to it. Which is why God instructs us to concern ourselves with it. We discern and discriminate in this most basic of physical enterprises because to do so when we are "most animalistic" demonstrates our ability to find the spark of holiness in every aspect of our beings.

Making the command "to be holy" apply to the most basic of what we do as *physical beings*, God demonstrates that it is the <u>process</u> of discriminating, of discerning, of *l'havdil* which elevates us. If we can restrain ourselves, turn away from the endless banquet; if we can most truly be "what we eat" then we have allowed our most basic, physical aspect to be imbued with holiness.

We have, at the most elemental level, distinguished ourselves from the beasts of the fields for we have distinguished ourselves at a point in our nature that is equal to theirs. By doing so, we bring holiness to the most basic of behaviors.

According to Rabbi Shneur Zalman of Liady, "in order to broaden his heart to God and His Torah, or in order to fulfill the *mitzvah* of pleasure on the Shabbat and *Yom Tov* … then that flesh has been affected by a measure of radiance, and goes up to the Almighty as a sacrifice." In other words, if a man eats with a mind (and soul!) toward God and His Torah then he actually *transforms* the flesh that he is eating. He has elevated it into more than simply a meal to satisfy his base hunger.

He has elevated it into a sacrifice to the Almighty.

To Separate –

It is interesting that "kosher" has come to mean something more than food that is approved to be eaten. "Kosher" has found its way into the lexicon of our society to mean something that is "right" or "appropriate." It is this sense that is understood when someone criticizes someone who has done something wrong by saying, "But that's not kosher."

While it is flattering as a Jew to see such a fundamental Jewish concept incorporated (in a good way) into modern understandings, it remains that *kashrut* has more to do with the Jewish concept of holiness than it does with what our society considers right or wrong.

I have established that, while we might find meaningful explanations for the various commandments regarding *kashrut*, ultimately, the reason that we keep *kashrut* is because God commands us to. And the only reason God gives us is that we are to be holy because God is holy.

In one sense, being holy is no different than any other command, or *mitzvah*. In another sense, it is wholly different. Every other *mitzvah* has very clearly defined parameters. Whether one kind of food is kosher, when *t'fillin* stops being *t'fillin*, what constitutes a "kosher" *etrog*, etc. However, the performance of any or all of these *mitvot* has a single purpose – to be holy.

But, what does it really *mean*, to be holy? Certainly we Jews are not the first or the only nation to ask this question. Many people have grappled with the idea of "being holy". Tragically, some of the most profound cruelties exacted on others have been done in the name of "holiness."

Does it not occur to anyone that "holy war" is an oxymoron? How many pogroms have been perpetrated on Jews? And why? Ultimately, to avenge a perceived injury to a religious faith. In other words, for "holiness."

While the world pursues its understanding of "holiness" perhaps it is worth our time to examine what is meant by that word. There is a direct connection between the English word "holy" and the word "halo." What can we learn from this connection? Clearly, Western cultures (the cultures from which English is derived) saw a connection between those who were pictured with halos and those who were holy. In other words, angels and saints.

Our non-Jewish neighbors speak of holiness in the context of saintly perfection. That is not the Jewish way. In Hebrew, the word for "holy" is *kadosh*.

This word comes from the root, the *shoresh*, koof, dalet, shin. This root means "to separate."

In other words, to discriminate, to choose, to "set apart."

God's call for us to be holy is a call to be set apart. In other words, to set limits and to say, no, to the infinite possibilities that the world presents to us because in that saying "no" we find the discipline to fan the flames of holiness that exist within us.

Which brings us back, in an interesting way, not only to the idea of "separation" but *what* we choose to separate. Other religions and philosophies, both Western and Eastern, seek "holiness" and enlightenment by separating the body from the soul. In the process, they necessarily deny the fundamental goodness of God's creation.

As Jews, we do not seek separation from our essential natures. We recognize that anything that God created is necessarily good. It is by our relation with each part of creation that we affirm its goodness and holiness.

*Kashrut*, by focusing on our universal, animal need to eat, affirms the connection, the absolute *kesher* between the physical and the spiritual. Our discipline, our discrimination – our separation – is a discipline which reminds us of the holiness of creation, our own role and our relationship with our creator.

For I Am Holy –

*Kashrut* teaches us that the Jewish view of holiness and spiritually is intimately related to the physical substance of life. It is impossible to divorce oneself from the world and the physical reality of life and be in pursuit of genuine holiness and spirituality. Judaism teaches that the first commandment delivered to man was to "be fruitful and multiply." By definition, if God has delivered such a commandment to man then the fulfillment of the commandment *must* bring one closer to God, which is the very definition of spirituality.

I think it bears repeating that fulfilling this commandment demands that we engage in the most basic of human physical interactions. And it is good.

As I have tried to make clear throughout this essay, the various *mitzvot* that concern themselves with *kashrut* make very clear the essential connection between body and soul, emphasizing that the relationship between the two is like a marriage in that the union of the two enlarges and enriches each individually.

So, in Judaism "holiness" is anything but a retreat from the world. It is, in fact, an embrace of the physical world that God has created and deemed to be good. But, it is an embrace that is defined in very specific ways in order to be appropriate.

Jews are distinguished from the other peoples of the world not by the "rules" – *mishpatim* – that we observe. Our sages teach us that the *mishpatim* are human rules, rules that would most likely have evolved naturally from human interaction if God had not delivered them to us. No, it is not the *mishpatim* that sets us apart but the *chukim*, the laws that God has commanded us to observe.

Our tradition teaches us that the *chukim* have no rational reason as such. While it should be self-evident that it does not benefit man or society when murder and thievery is allowed, it is not so evident that the laws of *kashrut* provide a similar benefit. In other words, left to our own devices, we would not have come up with the laws of *kashrut*.

Put another way, *mishpatim* are rules that concern themselves with the interaction of people with other people. *Chukim* are the laws that govern the relationship between the individual and God.

In defining Jews as a "holy people" God's laws serve as the template to show *how* to be holy. For that is the call to every Jew, to be holy for "I, the Lord your God, am holy."

How then are we to *be* holy?

Our sages often concerned themselves with such questions in all manner of context. For example, there are many prayers in our liturgy, communal prayers, that can only be recited as a community. Most people would acknowledge an intuitive understanding of what it means to have "communal prayer." But an intuitive understanding is not sufficient when it comes to making sure that God's directives are met. So our sages asked, "what is a community?" – not, mind you, in the philosophic sense of what makes a community distinctive, its rules, mores, traditions, location, etc. No, the rabbis sought a more elemental – down to earth, if you will – definition. They wanted to know, How many people have to be gathered together to be able to say that a community has gathered?

Certainly if a thousand people are together, we can say that the numbers are sufficient to form a community but what if only five hundred are gathered? Or one hundred? Fifty?

In other words, what is the fewest number of people (and what characteristics must these people have by dint of age, gender, etc.) to form a prayer community? The rabbis settled on the number ten, which every Jew will recognize as the number of men needed to form a *minyan*.

I offer this insight into the definition of a *minyan* because it goes to the heart of what it means for a Jew to be holy. It means to, perhaps, intuit the need for holiness and then to grapple with very real, very specific aspects of how that "holiness" looks and behaves *in the world*.

We Jews, you see, take God's word very seriously.

For example, in the *v'ahavta* prayer, we are told to "place these words which I command you this day upon your heart... bind them as a sign between your eyes, and you shall inscribe them upon the doorposts of your house and upon your gates."

Now, as beautiful and poetic as these words are, our sages do not read them as poetry but as a specific instruction – to take the words God commanded and "place them" upon our hearts and to "bind them as a sign between" our eyes. But... *how?* "How" is the essential Jewish question. "Why?" is a given, because God instructed it.

We are to be holy. That is not to be questioned.

*How* to be holy... ah, that becomes our life's work.

In addressing the "how" of the above commandment, the Torah devised two ritual objects of exceeding beauty and brilliance – *tefillin* and *mezzuzot*. By using these two objects as proscribed, an individual Jew fulfills literally the commandments of God and becomes, by definition, holy.

One aspect of the rules of *kashrut* that distinguishes them from being simply rules "about what to eat" is the ethical aspect. For example, in addition to rules about what can and cannot be eaten, the rules of *kashrut* forbids the mixing of dairy and meat together. The genesis of this prohibition is the verse in Deuteronomy:

> *You shall not eat of any thing that dies of itself; you shall give it to the stranger that is in your gates, that he may eat it; or you may sell it to a foreigner; for you are a holy people to the Lord your God. You shall not boil a kid in its mother's milk.*

While the "simple meaning" of this prohibition, which appears two other times in the book of Exodus, is fairly apparent, but it has been expanded

upon greatly by our rabbinic tradition. The extension of this law, by apply-
ing the rabbinic tradition of "building a fence around the Torah," results in the
prohibition of mixing milk and meat products.

There is the suggestion that this prohibition exists because, at the time we
were in the desert, there were a number of idolatrous people from whom we
sought to distinguish ourselves. There is the suggestion that there was a common pagan sacrificial practice to offer a fetal or newborn goat boiled in the
milk of its mother. This was considered an abomination by the Israelites.

There is ample reason to consider this explanation reasonable. However, reasonable or not, it would be unsatisfactory. Just as the explanations
for *kashrut* which sought validity in suggesting that the laws of *kashrut* were
in place for health reasons was not satisfactory, so too is this. For such an
explanation presumes that the rules of *kashrut* are *mishpatim* rather than
*chukim*.

We derive meaning – and holiness – from *chukim* not by "explaining" them
but in placing ourselves in holy relationship to them. We derive meaning from
them. We don't "outthink" them. Perhaps the sage Ibn Ezra gives us the best
insight into understanding this prohibition – and understanding how it helps
us to "be holy."

Ibn Ezra makes the connection between the injunction not to boil a kid in
its mother's milk to two other Torah injunctions – not to slaughter a cow and
her offspring on the same day (Leviticus 22:28) and not to take a mother bird
from the nest along with her eggs. (Deuteronomy 22:6-7).

Clearly, this great sage saw a profound commonality in these three edicts
– to kill a mother and her offspring at the same time demonstrates a profound
lack of sensitivity to life itself. In other words, there is a very real ethical – holy
– dynamic at play. By not mixing milk and meat (which, ultimately presents
the *possibility* that we would be eating the meat of a kid along with the mother's
milk) we are adhering to basic and fundamental laws about the integrity and
dignity of life.

Be holy.

We see this same concern in the rules and practices of *Shechita*, of the ritual slaughter of animals to be eaten. While a fundamental goal in preparing
an animal to be eaten is to remove the blood from the body – for the blood
is the life – the *method* of killing is such to minimize any suffering of the ani-

mal. In other words, Judaism teaches implicitly that there is dignity to life *even when the rules and practices for the slaughter of an animal are being defined.*

Be holy.

To be holy in Judaism is to unite the physical and the spiritual in a marriage of dignity and respect. To be holy in Judaism is to *behave* in a holy manner. As they do in every other matter, our sages accepted this precept, that to be holy is to behave in a holy manner, and they asked, How?

What exactly do we do, or not do?

Chapter 19 in the Book of Leviticus, the text often referred to as the "holiness code" gives us an idea.

*And the Lord spoke to Moses, saying, Speak to all the congregation of the people of Israel, and say to them, You shall be holy; for I the Lord your God am holy. You shall revere every man his mother, and his father, and keep my Sabbaths; I am the Lord your God. Turn you not to idols, nor make to yourselves molten gods; I am the Lord your God. And if you offer a sacrifice of peace offerings to the Lord, you shall offer it of your own will. It shall be eaten the same day you offer it, and on the next day; and if anything remains until the third day, it shall be burned in the fire. And if it is eaten at all on the third day, it is abominable; it shall not be accepted. Therefore every one who eats it shall bear his iniquity, because he has profaned the consecrated thing of the Lord; and that soul shall be cut off from among his people. And when you reap the harvest of your land, you shall not reap to the very corners of your field, nor shall you gather the gleanings of your harvest. And you shall not glean your vineyard, nor shall you gather every grape of your vineyard; you shall leave them for the poor and stranger; I am the Lord your God. You shall not steal, nor deal falsely, nor lie one to another. And you shall not swear by my name falsely, nor shall you profane the name of your God; I am the Lord. You shall not defraud your neighbor, nor rob him; the wages of he who is hired shall not remain with you all night until the morning. You shall not curse the deaf, nor put a stumbling block before the blind, but shall fear your God; I am the Lord. You shall do no unrighteousness in judgment; you shall not respect the person of the poor, nor honor the person of the mighty; but in righteousness shall you judge your neighbor. You shall not go up and down as a slanderer among your people; nor shall you stand against the blood of your neighbor; I am the Lord. You shall not hate your brother in your heart; you shall reason with your neighbor, and not allow sin on his account. You shall not avenge, nor bear any grudge against the children of your people, but you shall love your neighbor as yourself; I am the Lord. You shall keep my statutes. You shall not let your cattle breed with a different kind; you shall not sow your field with mixed seed; nor shall a garment mixed of linen and woolen come upon you. And whoever lies carnally with a woman, who is a slave betrothed to a man, and not wholly redeemed, nor freedom given her; inquiry shall be made; they shall not be put to death, because she was not free. And he shall bring his guilt offering to the Lord, to the door of the Tent of Meeting, a ram for a guilt offering. And the priest shall make an atonement for him with the ram of the guilt offering before the Lord for his sin which he has done; and the sin which he has done shall be forgiven him. And when you shall come into the land, and shall have planted all kinds of trees for food, then you shall count its fruit as uncircumcised; three years shall it be uncircumcised to you; it shall not be eaten. But in the fourth year all its fruit shall be holy for praise giving to the Lord. And in the fifth year shall you eat of its fruit, that it may yield to you its produce; I am the Lord your God. You shall not eat any thing with the blood; nor shall you use enchantment, nor observe times. You shall not round the corners of your heads, nor shall you mar the corners of your beard. You shall not make any cuttings in your flesh for the dead, nor print any marks upon you; I am the Lord. Do not prostitute your daughter, to cause her to be a harlot; lest the land fall to harlotry, and the land become full of wickedness. You shall keep my Sabbaths, and reverence my sanctuary; I am the Lord. Regard not those who are mediums, nor seek after wizards, to be defiled by them; I am the Lord your God. You shall rise up before the hoary head, and honor the face of the old man, and fear your God; I am the Lord. And if a stranger sojourns with you in your land, you shall not wrong him. But the stranger who dwells with you shall be to you as one born among you, and you shall love him as yourself; for you were strangers in the land of Egypt; I am the Lord your God. You shall do no unrighteousness in judgment, in measures of length, of weight, or quantity. Just balances, just weights, a just ephah, and a just hin, shall you have; I am the Lord your God, which brought you out of the land of Egypt. Therefore shall you observe all my statutes, and all my judgments, and do them; I am the Lord.*

While some of these rules are familiar to all, some bear closer attention. "Just balances, just weights…" In other words, behave ethically. "Do not put a stumbling block before the blind…" In other words, do not take advantage of vulnerabilities and weaknesses. The injunction not to harvest "to the very corners" is so the poor are able to eat, and not only eat but to *earn* their food by their labor.

Holiness demands dignity, dignity of spirit and of body.

Be holy.

To be Jewish is to be holy. And, as we have learned, to be holy is to *engage* the physical, not to divorce ourselves from it. *Kashrut* is a fundamental and regular way of engaging the physical in a way that reminds us of the holy.

# Addendum*

KOSHER SPECIES

1. Animals

The Torah (Leviticus 11:3) lists the characteristics of permitted animals as those with fully split hooves, who also chew their cud (ruminants). Kosher animals are always mammals and herbivores. The kosher animals commonly eaten today are the cow, goat and sheep – and sometimes deer and buffalo.

2. Birds

The Torah enumerates 24 forbidden species of birds, and the Talmud explains that, among other signs, all birds of prey (vulture, hawk, eagle) are forbidden. In practice today, we eat only those birds for which there is an established tradition that the bird is kosher – e.g. chicken, turkey, duck and goose.

As for "kosher eggs," they must come from a species of kosher bird (e.g. chicken).

3. Fish

The Torah (Leviticus 11:9) teaches that a kosher fish must possess both fins and scales. (Fins help the fish swim, and scales are a covering over the body.) Even if the fish has only one scale or one fin, it is permitted. Tuna, for example, have very few scales, yet is kosher. Other popular kosher fish are bass, carp, cod, flounder, halibut, herring, mackerel, trout and salmon.

*Source: ABCs of Kosher, by Rabbi Shraga Simmons-Aish.com

Crustaceans (such as lobster and crab) and other shellfish (such as clams) are not kosher, because they lack scales. Further, all aquatic mammals (e.g. whales and dolphins) are not kosher.

And yes, there are kosher varieties of sushi and caviar – providing it's from a kosher species (fins and scales), and that it was prepared only with kosher utensils (knife, cutting board, etc.).

### 4. Insects

Many are surprised to discover that four species of grasshoppers are kosher (Leviticus 11:22). However, all other insects are not kosher. One might think that this has little practical application to our modern eating habits. But in truth, many leafy vegetables (lettuce, broccoli) often contain insects and must be carefully examined before they can be eaten. Some fruits like raspberries and strawberries are also problematic. Rabbis have developed specific methods to properly check these fruits and vegetables for insects.

## KOSHER SLAUGHTERING

### 1. Shechita

Besides being from a kosher species, kosher meat requires that the animal/bird be slaughtered in the manner prescribed by the Torah (*Shechita*). (Fish do not have this requirement.) In this procedure, a trained kosher slaughterer (*shochet*) severs the trachea and esophagus of the animal with a special razor-sharp knife. . This also severs the jugular vein, causing near-instantaneous death with minimal pain to the animal.

### 2. Bedika

After the animal/bird has been properly slaughtered, its internal organs are inspected for any physiological abnormalities that may render the animal non-kosher (*treif*). The lungs, in particular, must be examined to determine that there are no adhesions (*sirchot*) which may be indicative of a puncture in the lungs.

### 3. Nikkur

Animals contain many veins (e.g. *Gid HaNashe*) and fats (*chelev*) that are forbidden by the Torah and must be removed. The procedure of removal is called "Nikkur," and it is quite complex. In practice today, the hind quarter of most kosher animals is simply removed and sold as non-kosher meat.

## 4. Salting

The Torah forbids eating of the blood of an animal or bird (Leviticus 7:26); fish do not have this requirement. Thus in order to extract the blood, the entire surface of meat must be covered with coarse salt. It is then left for an hour on an inclined or perforated surface to allow the blood to flow down freely. The meat is then thoroughly washed to remove all salt. Meat must be koshered within 72 hours after slaughter so as not to permit the blood to congeal. (An alternate means of removing the blood is through broiling on a perforated grate over an open fire.)

ADDITIONAL PROHIBITIONS

## 1. Meat and Milk

The Torah forbids eating meat and milk in combination, and even forbids the act of cooking them together (as well as deriving benefit from such a mixture). As a safeguard, the Sages disallow the eating of meat and dairy products at the same meal, or preparing them with the same utensils. Therefore, a kosher kitchen must have two separate sets of pots, pans, plates and silverware – one for meat/poultry and the other for dairy foods.

One must wait up to six hours after eating meat products before eating dairy products. However, meat may be eaten following dairy products (with the exception of hard cheese, which also requires a six-hour interval). Prior to eating meat after dairy, one must eat a solid food and the mouth must be rinsed.

## 2. Limb of Live Animal

The Torah (Deut. 12:23) prohibits eating a limb that was removed from an animal before it was killed. In Hebrew, this is called *Ever Min HaChai*. (This requirement is actually one of the Seven Noahide Laws that apply to non-Jews as well.)

## 3. Chalav Yisrael

A Rabbinic law requires that there be supervision during the milking process to ensure that the milk comes from a kosher animal. In the United States, many people rely on the Department of Agriculture's regulations and controls as sufficiently stringent to fulfill the rabbinic requirement for supervision. Many people, however, do not rely on this, and will only eat dairy products that are designated as *Chalav Yisrael* (literally, "Jewish milk").

## 4. Bishul Akum

*Bishul Akum* is a Hebrew term meaning, "cooked by a non-Jew." As a rabbinic safeguard against assimilation, certain foods cooked by a non-Jew are considered not kosher. While the details of this law are many, the basic rule is that any cooked food which: 1) could not have been eaten raw, and 2) is important enough to be served at a fancy meal table, may not be eaten if cooked by a non-Jew.

If a Jew assists with lighting the fire or the cooking, the food may be eaten even if it was cooked by a non-Jew (assuming, of course, that the food itself was kosher in every other way).

KOSHER PRODUCE

## 1. Grains

In keeping kosher, there is a grain-related issue called *Chadash* and *Yashan* – literally "new" and "old." The Torah (Leviticus 23:14) says that if a grain (such as wheat) was harvested *prior* to Passover, then we may not eat that grain until *after* (the second day of) Passover.

This means that we have two kinds of grain: grain that hasn't celebrated its first Passover is (temporarily) forbidden as *Chadash*, while grain that has been around long enough to already have a Passover under its belt is *Yashan*, and permitted to eat.

Another grain-related issue is *Challah*. (This is not to be confused with the braided bread that we eat on Shabbat.) When one kneads a significant amount of dough (over 2.5 pounds) for baking purposes, a small portion of the dough is removed and burned. (In the times of the Holy Temple, this portion was given to a Kohen.) Once challah has been separated from the larger dough, the dough is "kosher" for baking into bread or other items.

## 2. Fruits

Fruit that grows during the first three years after a tree is planted is called *Orlah* and is not kosher to be eaten. This law applies to trees both in Israel and the Diaspora. If you plant a fruit tree in your backyard, you cannot eat the fruit for three years, and there is a special procedure to render the fruit permissible to eat in the fourth year. (Consult with a rabbi.)

## 3. Israeli Produce

*Trumah* and *Maaser* are terms for various tithes that apply to Israeli-grown produce, to be given to the Kohen and Levi. Untithed foods are called *Tevel* and are not kosher to be eaten. If you're visiting Israel, or even if you're buy-ing Israeli oranges or tomatoes in your local supermarket, you should make sure that proper tithes have been taken from all grains, fruits and vegetables.

The Torah (Leviticus chapter 25) says that every seven years, agricultural work must cease in the Land of Israel. This is called *Shmita* – the seventh, sab-batical year. Produce that grows on land that was "farmed and worked" dur-ing the seventh year is not kosher. Today, with the return of a Jewish agricultural industry to Israel, the laws related to *Shmita* are once again very relevant. So if you're buying Israeli produce, make sure the laws of Shmita were properly observed.

# SAVE OUR CHILDREN

## A MEDITATION ON *TZNIUT*, THE TRADITIONAL JEWISH VIEW OF MODESTY

I must confess, on this matter of *tzniut* and the modern world, I could write a book. However, my meditation here must be a bit more circumspect.

We live in a time that rivals the fall of Rome in its essential immodesty. However, where Rome crumbled under its own overwrought sense of power and outrage, we have allowed immodesty to define the modern world almost as a matter of default. In the process, we have witnessed the necessary byproduct of immodesty – the dehumanization of our children and ourselves.

When we compromise what is meant by *tzniut*, we compromise something profound about who we are; we compromise something dear in our essential natures, something God-given.

I am mindful that there are those who would dismiss my outrage as being a bit "overwrought," or perhaps the predictable criticisms of an Orthodox rabbi. I wish the weakness and flaws of our modern culture could be so easily dismissed by a "kill the messenger" argument. Sadly, they cannot.

But, as they say on television, You don't have to take my word for it. Just look around. You would have to be willfully blind not to see that our children are at terrible risk. They are bombarded in the media and on the Internet with images of SEX, SEX, SEX twenty-four hours a day, seven days a week. Movies, music, and books idealize shallow relationships that mirror our disposable society. "Hooking up" is the new courtship. "Idealized" beauty images are causing our daughters – and sons – to degrade the magnificent bodies that God has given them. There are world famous fashion models that are starving themselves and dying before our eyes. The situation has become so dire that even the fashion community – hardly known for its concern for models – is beginning to take note, requiring models to have a minimum Body Mass Index before they can walk on the runways in Milan, Brazil, and Paris.

Yet, the models continue to waste away. They take on the appearance of, God forbid!, survivors as they were taken from the camps. And for what? Some idealized – and impossible and destructive - body form!

Perhaps we could look away if it were only a vain subset of our culture that was victimized by this damaging dynamic. But it is not just models who are killing themselves. Walk along the beach, or the shore of a lake, or a public swimming pool any summer afternoon and you will see young boys and girls parading around in bathing suits that would make an honest Madame blush.

Micro-bikinis.

Thongs.

Have we lost our last vestige of shame? What kind of a culture allows its children to parade about in public like that?

You might argue that my reaction to these kinds of images just proves my "lack of credentials" to speak to the issue; that I am hopelessly lost in the past and I don't "understand" the modern world. Your argument might have some validity if this was about me. But it's not. It is about our children and the terrible toll that these behaviors are taking on them.

Listen. Can't you hear them crying out for our help? Look at them. Don't you see the tears in their eyes? We have denied our children their basic humanity. The simple fact is, our children have been turned into commodities – lumps of flesh, seemingly formed for no other purpose than the buying and selling of product.

And shame on us for then bemoaning the fact that they don't have self-respect or positive self-images. The world – our world, the world our generation has created – demands too much. Our children wear the finest – if skimpiest – clothes. They study at the best universities. They live in the biggest houses and drive in the most expensive automobiles. They vacation in resorts. They celebrate birthdays with parties more elaborate than their parents' wedding.

They've "got it all." And they've got nothing. For, I ask you, where in all this do we talk about the soul? About God? When and where do we raise our children up instead of participating in making the world and their experience of it more difficult? When do we build a fence around them to *protect* them from the bombardment of the modern world rather than insistently expose them to the worst the world has to throw their way?

You ask me, what can an Orthodox rabbi tell me about the perils of this culture and the threat it poses to our children? Plenty.

The Talmud, the compendium of Jewish law and wisdom, teaches that "a person is led in the direction he wants to follow." So now, I will answer this question with a more important question: What direction would you choose for yourself and your children?

If you would choose a safe, more sane and ennobling direction for you and them, then I would (modestly!) suggest that an Orthodox rabbi has quite a bit to tell you about life – whether you're an observant Jew, a non-practicing Jew, or not a Jew at all.

Long ago, when one of the great Jewish sages, Rabbi Hillel, was challenged to teach the complete Torah while standing on one foot, he was non-plussed. He replied simply that the whole of the Torah is, "not doing anything to one's neighbor that one would not have his neighbor do to him."

It seems almost too simple to be worth considering in our complex world, that the complete teaching of Torah could be distilled in this simple concept: if you don't want it done to you, don't do it to someone else. We talk dismissively about "sound bites" but could any truth be rendered more succinctly? It's so simple as to be dismissible. But we turn away from this ethical eloquence – and its importance to *tzniut* – at our own peril.

In giving such an answer, Hillel accomplished an incredible goal. He affirmed the sanctity and authority of the Torah as an ethical guide by which to negotiate the too-often Byzantine maze of the world. Judaism has often been described as being defined by rules, as being "legalistic." It is true. We have many specific rules to guide us in all manner of life and in all sorts of situations. However, underlying all of these rules is the essential truth that Hillel captured in his answer and, more importantly, the relationship that we have with God.

How we behave in the world – how we face "outward" – is a question of ethics. How we behave in matters of holiness – how we face "inward" – is essentially a question of morals.

*Tzniut* is the nexus where the outward and the inward intersect. It is the reality that informs both.

Wise King Solomon, son of King David, wrote in the Book of Proverbs, "Can a man take fire into his bosom and his clothes not be burned?" His poetic language makes clear that a man cannot be one thing on the inside and something else on the outside. A man's heart and soul cannot be fouled while he maintains the appearance of purity and piety.

However, just as a man with an unclear heart and soul cannot present an outward holiness and purity to the world, the opposite is also true. A person whose appearance in the world – whose outward appearance – is without purity and piety can not possibly be pure of heart and soul. The outward and the inward go hand in hand. Certainly, they do in the person who is, to quote the modern philosopher and psychologist, Abraham Maslow, self-actualized. We fragment ourselves at our peril, believing that it is possible to be ruthless at work and gentle at home or unfair in the marketplace but fair in matters of personal conduct. Modern medicine and psychology has only begun to genuinely respect that there is a very real mind-body connection when it comes to disease and healing. Judaism has known about the connection for several thousands of years.

*Tzniut* is the interchange, the nexus, between the ethical and the moral, between the inward-facing and the outward-facing.

Although many people dismiss *tzniut* as little more than a "dress code" we will come to understand that *tzniut*, modesty, is not a cloak that hides beauty but a posture that defines and displays what is *more beautiful*. It is not an action but a perspective; not an appearance but rather a way of being that has direct bearing not only on how we live but on who we are.

And *that*, my friends, has everything to do with you, with your children, with the world in which we find ourselves; it has everything to do with the wisdom that Judaism has been passing down from generation to generation for hundreds upon hundreds of years. It has everything to do with what an Orthodox rabbi can teach you. And, as you will discover, it has everything to do with your life, and your children's lives.

When you look around at the natural world you see, in the broadest sense, things – objects, shapes, colors. These various objects take on greater or lesser clarity depending on your perspective. Physical details are more or less visible, depending on your visual acuity, where you stand in proximity to the object and the instrument you use to view the object. In other words, "seeing" is a physical function. It is a property of physics, the way that light moves, and biology, the way our eyes interpret that movement of light.

*Tzniut* is not a physical function and, as such, it requires a different way of looking, of seeing.

In an everyday sense, we see things in the most superficial sense. When we look at a flag rippling on a flagpole, we see the cloth, with its colors and design, flapping in the breeze. We see a rigid pole rising into the sky. When we walk along the sidewalk, we might look at the structures lining the street. A small shop, with a large window and a display inside. An apartment building, with its brick façade, windows and broad stoop. We look at a tree and we see its trunk, its leaves and its limbs.

In short, we look at the object and we see its physical properties.

We look at a young woman on the street and we see her eyes, her hair, her height, her physical attributes, the clothes she is wearing. We look at a young man and we see how tall he is, how muscular, whether or not he has a mustache or a strong jaw.

We look at a person and we see a collection of his or her parts.

However, as is the case in all things, everyone and everything is much, much more than the sum of its, or their, parts. There are infinite aspects to every thing and every person. *Tzniut* challenges us to see more than simply the surface.

Take, for example, that flag rippling in the breeze. One person might gaze upon it and see the promise of a nation. Another might feel overwhelmed with emotions from an experience in the military. Yet another might react to his feelings about a particular political dynamic. In other words, it is possible to react to a flag and see just about anything *but* its physical dimension.

Do the same thing in another context. Picture yourself walking along that sidewalk again only this time, when you look over and see the apartment building, picture instead that you are looking at the apartment where your grandparents lived. What do you see now?

Do you see people who loved you very much; people who stood at the doorway and waved to you whenever you went away? Do you smell the aroma of wonderful meals that your grandmother cooked for you? Do you see the gathering of family for holidays and special occasions?

That apartment building is no longer "just" an apartment building, is it? It is more than the sum of its windows, doors and stoop. It is the repository of memories. In short, it is not a house. It is a home.

When we are honest, we know that the physical is never *just* the physical. We must also factor in our complete experience and interaction with the physical. And this often means our engagement of it on anything but a superficial level.

The fundamental – and relevant – lesson that the Talmud teaches is that in order to truly hear and accept moral and ethical precepts and teachings, it is necessary to hold the proper perspective about the body and soul. A man's scholarship and wisdom is not directly related to his physical beauty however, the degree of a man's wisdom is directly related to his <u>attitude</u> about beauty. A handsome man who does not value his beauty will not be swayed by vanity and become proud or arrogant.

The traditional view regarding our physical nature is that everything physical about us, including our beauty, is a gift given to us by God when we were born. Nothing in our behavior or decisions, nothing in our virtue, brought it about. Wisdom, morals, ethics – human decency – these are the things that we are called upon to acquire and develop *according to our choices and our abilities.*

The physical is a given. The often *unseen* is the aspect of life which we must nurture. Could this traditional view stand in greater contrast to the modern view that it is *physical beauty* and sexual attractiveness that are the assets that will bring about the most benefits and positives?

Or, put another way, What do we value in the modern world – the house or the home? Have we limited our ability to see to only those things most superficial?

Too often, it seems so. The so-called "McMansions" would certainly suggest that we are more interested in the house rather than the home. But this trivializing of experience is not limited to architecture. One needs only to listen to popular music, watch modern television programs, go to the movies, and be bombarded by advertising to know that we have reduced most human interaction to the most superficial. In honesty, when was the last time you saw an advertisement that did not appeal to your most base instincts?

Sex sells, right?

Perhaps it does. But then that begs the question, If Sex sells, what exactly is being sold? I would suggest that it is you and me. It is not only the "product" that is being advertised but also everyone and everything involved in the transaction – the models and actors, the advertising executive, the CEO, the packaging artist and you and me. We are all co-conspirators in this process that reduces us to two-dimensional caricatures articulated ultimately by the sensibility (or lack thereof!) of advertisers.

Think of the necessary implications of this – rather than being the crown of God's creation, the attitude of the advertisers and the acquiescence of consumers turns us all into base creatures, motivated by our appetites rather than our souls. When our souls are removed from the equation, we really *are* reduced to little more than the sum of our parts.

But such a reduction of what we are as human beings is unfathomable. We human beings are the most multifaceted creature in all of creation. Reducing any of us to a caricature of two dimensions is foolhardy and, in a real sense, impossible. It is true that, upon meeting someone for the first time, we might "identify" her by her physical attributes.

She was tall.

She had brown eyes.

Her hair was curly.

She was wearing black shoes.

However, it does not take much time for a more complete image to develop.

She was "funny" or "musical."

As time goes on, the image continues to develop. She becomes "empathetic" or "high strung." However that picture gets filled in, it *does* get filled in.

The modern world may resist any sense of you except the most superficial but we can never really be reduced to only the superficial. We are too much more. But, how to protect that "too much more"?

The culture begins to rob us of our ability to appreciate the subtleties, complexities and depth of one another almost from the moment we can walk. We lose the ability to see the true beauty of one another and, in losing that, how we really are. So, how do we regain our ability to see people "as they really are" rather than merely "how they look?"

Ironically, *tzniut* would have us begin by looking in the mirror.

Literally.

Take a moment to look at yourself in the mirror. What do you see? Do you see only your most superficial characteristics? The color of your eyes? Your nose and lips? Do you see laugh lines? Worry lines?

What about those eyes and that nose? Are they your mother's eyes? Your father's nose? Do you recall their eyes gazing at you when you were young?

Do you see the person who first thought about God and how you are supposed to live your life? Do you see the joy of being a parent or a grandparent?

Can you begin to see the person *within*?

Looking within means to look – and see – more deeply than just the surface. And, of course, by this I don't mean more deeply into the *physical* aspect of your looks. I mean to look more deeply into the *being* that animates the physical presence that is you. When you begin to do that, you are beginning to grasp what *tzniut* means.

*Tzniut* means looking more deeply. While its more conventional and simplistic translation, "modesty," fails to fully capture the fullness of what *tzniut* means, the exercise of looking more deeply is a good start. By looking deeper than your most superficial, corporeal self and seeing who you are at your deeper levels you are also able to see the person you are capable of being. And *that* person is the one that God wants you to be, the one who does not do to others what he wouldn't want done to him.

In addition, *tzniut* is the process of taking this deeper self and making *it* the one that is discernable to others; so that when someone looks at you, they don't see your hair color or your height or the shoes you are wearing – they don't see the superficial and the corporeal first – but they see your essential goodness first and foremost.

*Tzniut* requires that you see – and are seen – through new eyes so that you can see the person who must shine through to others, and they can see it too.

The call of *tzniut* is a call to look inward, to see who you are (or can be) and then to find a way to make that part of you the *you* that people recognize, not the clothes that some fashion designer would have you wear or the hair style some celebrity is currently wearing. You.

In the Book of Proverbs, Solomon notes, "A good name is more desirable than great riches, a good reputation more than silver or gold." Perhaps the Talmud says it best, "In your town, it is your name that counts. In another, it is your clothes." Where people know you, your outward appearance is less important than the person that they have come to know over the years. When people first meet you, they have no choice but to confront your physical presence first. *Tzniut* suggests that your physical presence immediately call attention to your better, inner self rather than just to itself.

Imagine how much more comfortable our children would be in their bodies (or, put another way, how much greater their self-esteem would be) if they were not constantly *competing* for an idealized physical appearance and instead had only to present themselves in a way that reflected the goodness that is within them, the goodness that God put there! If we could instill this sense of modesty, of *tzniut*, in our children I dare say that many of the problems that they struggle with, problems like eating disorders or substance abuse or psychological disorders, would simply melt away because many of these problems are nothing more than symptoms of the relentless focus our culture forces them to place on their outward selves rather than their inward selves.

How foolish our constant drive for mere physical attractiveness! The futility and vanity of it should be obvious if only as a practical matter. As the ancients understood, "Beauty diminishes, but a good name endures." Even in an age of gym memberships, Botox, and plastic surgery, beauty fades. An older woman who has obviously "had work done" is not youthful or beautiful. She is a mockery of the person she could and should be. Her "good name" is lost to the futile efforts to stave off what cannot be staved off to begin with. The relentless efforts some people display to "hold on" to their youthful looks or physical beauty turn them into physical caricatures as well as make clear that their good names are not of great interest to them.

Your appearance should "display" your best qualities, not hide them.

Sadly, in our culture, too many people consider their best qualities to be their most superficial. They cloak themselves in possessions. They drape their bodies in clothes that do not even belong in the bedroom! Ironically, their immodest dress actually serves to cloak that which should be revealed and to reveal that which should be cloaked! The task of *tzniut* then is to reverse this self-defeating dynamic. It allows you to display your wonderful, God-given qualities, by *not* displaying that which shouldn't be displayed.

Isn't that a marvelous insight, That by *hiding* that which should be hidden the necessary consequence is to display that which should be displayed?

Of course, with all this talk about revealing your true self, you might be asking, "What is my true self?" Or, put another way, "Who am I?" This is, of course, the essential question that we must ask because it is only by virtue of the answer that *tzniut* has any real meaning other than "just another fashion statement."

According to Jewish tradition, each one of us possesses a spark of God. That is our soul. That is the essential part of ourselves that we must nurture. It is goodness. It is humility. It is the ability to live according to Hillel's precept: not to do to another what you would not have them do to you.

Your essential self is one of well-deserved self-respect. Well-deserved? You may ask why it is well-deserved if it has been given to you by no effort of your own. It is well-deserved because God has seen fit to give it to you and God does not give such gifts unless they are deserved. Your self-respect is what God has given you and preserved for you. According to one of the famous books of Jewish mysticism, the Zohar, "God conceals himself from the mind of man, but reveals himself to his heart."

Could there be a better guide to the essential self than that? The sad reality of life is that we stray *away* from this simple truth. By our actions in the world, we sometimes lose the ability to see who we really are. *Tzniut* is the process for rediscovering ourselves and letting that be what we show to the world, rather than the confused wayfarer we've become.

Each of us possesses a soul, a spark of God. This is truth. This is why *tzniut* means so much more than a dress code. For too many, *tzniut* represents nothing more than dress and appearance; the "flip side" of immodest dress, true, but still nothing more. For these people, *tzniut* represents nothing more than long dresses and head scarves. (Others, more familiar with Orthodox Jewish communities, might also think of a *sheitel*, a wig that a married woman wears in order to cover her own, natural hair.)

But if these images are all that *tzniut* means, then they fall far short of a true understanding of *tzniut*. While it is true that appearance plays a significant role in how we understand *tzniut* that is because appearance is a significant component of modesty. After all, the wine must be contained in a vessel. Otherwise, it is nothing more than a spilled fluid. The vessel is extremely important. It is vital. Without it, the wine cannot exist in any meaningful way. But as the writer of Proverbs asks us, "Can a man take fire in his bosom and his clothes not be burned?" A good vessel is not enough though. A beautiful vessel can hold rancid wine. It is possible that even modest dress can be burned by an unholy fire in the bosom.

*Tzniut* is often found paired to the Jewish concept of *anavah*, or humility. This pairing is natural. The Talmud teaches that the reason that man was created on the last day of creation was so that his pride could be tempered. After all, had God not created even the insignificant gnat before him? We should all walk through life with a "light step" and be humble in character. The rabbis teach us this lesson in very direct terms. They teach that we should "be very humble in spirit because in the end you will be eaten by worms."

So, it should be obvious that one cannot be modest without being humble. However, it would be incorrect to think that *tzniut* and *anavah* are synonyms that can be used interchangeably. *Anavah* is a counterweight to haughtiness. As such, it has little bearing on a full understanding of *tzniut*. It is true that to be modest is to be humble in spirit, but humility is but a single shade on the coloring of *tzniut's* brilliant rainbow. To rely too much on this simple connection between the two is to miss the fullness of *tzniut's* meaning.

Yes, *tzniut* is modesty. It does affect the way we should behave, speak, dress, engage in relationships, understand ourselves. But to dwell too much on the simple outward manifestation of *tzniut* is to find ourselves engaged in the fundamental problem of those whose lives are lived far from modesty. A true and meaningful discussion of *tzniut* requires us to step *outside* the general discourse. *Tzniut* is not simply a variation of dress. It is a way of being that is reflected most obviously in how one dresses!

The problem with immoral dress is not the display of flesh *as such*. It is that, by this display, we are communicating an embrace of the superficial, the physical, the profane. It is not the "fleshiness" of the display that is the fundamental problem but the "outwardness" of the focus.

It should come as no surprise that this issue is not restricted to our own culture. In any culture where the focus is on spirituality and inwardness there will

be a similar emphasis on modesty, modest dress and the significance of either in a larger society. There was an article recently in the New York *Times*
in which young Muslim women in Egypt have turned their head coverings
(expressions of modesty in their culture) into little more than fashion statements. This is perfect example of the *trappings* of modesty being mistaken for
the real thing. When religious garb is worn in a way to call attention to itself,
that is, to be fashionable, then it is no better than the immodest dress that it
presumes to replace! There is no "otherness" in the discussion. Indeed, there
is the very real danger of haughtiness (which is the opposite of humility!)
where someone wears more modest dress and presumes that they are "better"
than someone who does not when, in fact, their intentions make them no better at all.

*Tzniut* is NOT a fashion statement. If it were, then it would do little to really
address the deeper problems of our children in our modern world. It would
be, quite literally, simply putting a new set of clothes on those problems.

*Tzniut* – being modest – is not simply a matter of outward appearances, of
dress. It is fundamentally more than that. It is not *dressing* modestly. It is not
*being* modest. It *is* modesty.

Modesty. I have been touting this quality as being fundamental to a meaningful life and yet the term itself presents us with a curious problem. If we
were to look up the word "modest" in a dictionary, we would discover that it
has not just a connotation of weakness but it *actually delineates* something less
than excellent, or weakness; as in, "he had modest skills." According to our
modern usage of the term, modesty actually *diminishes* that which it charac-
terizes! Yet, nothing could be further from the Jewish understanding of *tzniut*.
Jewish texts and tradition read into *tzniut* great strength. Some Jewish authors
even define *tzniut* as *g'vurah* – strength. In this, they have a long tradition. The
sages wrote, "Who is strong? He who conquers his *yetzer* (impulses or incli-
nations)."

A Hasidic Master taught that, "man's great guilt does not lie in the sins he
commits, for temptation is great and his strength limited. Man's great guilt lies
in the fact that he can turn away from evil at any moment, and yet he does
not." The ability to "turn away from evil", to resist an impulse, is at the heart
of what Judaism means by being modest.

When cast in this light, it should be clear that being modest is no task for the faint of heart, not dismissed as being merely a "woman's concern." In fact, in traditional Jewish texts the need to conquer temptation – to be a *tzanua* (a derivative from the same language root as *tzniut*) – is always cast in the masculine. All too often, when we think of *tzniut* we think of it being a feminine attribute. When we think about "modest dress" we invariably think of how women dress. When we think of modest behavior, we think of how women should act. Because our culture emphasizes the sexuality of women in fashion and body image, it is not surprising that we often see the response to this demeaning dynamic as a women's issue. But it is not. Our inward-most selves, the spark of God, has no gender in the way we perceive it. *Tzniut* is not a female issue or a male issue. It is a human issue.

Our shortsightedness in this regard is a terrible shortcoming because an important aspect of *tzniut* has to do with appropriate relationships between the sexes. To think that only one part in that relationship is responsible for modest thought and behavior is wrong. Traditional Jews maintain a separation between men and women in prayer services. It is true that one of the reasons for this is so that women don't become a distraction for a man at prayer. Still, it is as much an obligation on the man *not to be distracted* as it is on the woman not to be a distraction.

Equality between the sexes is very much a modern day social issue. To the surprise of many, gender equality has long been a concern of Judaism. However, it would be overly simplistic to think "equality" is nothing more than sameness. Judaism has always taught that the relationship between men and women must be defined by respect – that both parties are equally worthy of respect.

In this regard, the Zohar notes that the "ideal man has the strength of a male and the compassion of a female." According to the great Jewish thinker, Nachmanides, it is forbidden for a husband to force his wife to meet his sexual demands because the Spirit of the Divine is never with the mate who has sexual relations without real desire, love and free will.

Has any modern attempt to legislate equality between the sexes spoken more directly to the fundamental worth of each? Has any "politically correct" stance about the role and place of women in society spoken more clearly about the absolute obligation for respect and honor to be rendered equally between the sexes?

If "equality" is only seen as "sameness" – as in the same material options and the same salary then it loses a great deal of significance and meaning.

The question then presents itself, Why are clothes so important to how we understand modesty, or *tzniut*? Clothes are like a costume we wear to "get in the role" of who we really think we are. If we dress modestly, we are telling ourselves that we *are* modest. When we dress in clothes that could only be called immodest, we are telling ourselves that we do not possess the inner beauty and worth that deserves to be the priority of all that we do.

Even the most secular person understands the feeling of seeing clothing that he or she would "never put on" not even when alone in the privacy of his or her own room. Why not? Invariably, the answer will be some variation of, "Those clothes just aren't me." But what does that mean? Clothes are "just cloth." Aren't they? But of course they aren't. We all understand – and feel – that there is a real connection between how we present ourselves to the world and who we are.

The clothing aspect of *tzniut* holds that by dressing modestly, we can affect our inner modesty. In other words, it might start with clothing but it surely doesn't end there! What is essential to your experience with *tzniut* is whether you want the way you present yourself to the world to be defined by what you are on the inside or the outside. If you choose to dress so that your clothes draw attention to your physical presence, your body, the message you send out is, "Look at my body. I am a physical being." But if you choose to dress so that your clothes draw attention to your inner self, then the message you send out is, "I am a spiritual person. I care about my relationship with God and with the world." Ultimately, everyone but particularly Jews must devote their energy to that inner dimension of who they are, to their essence. They must ask themselves, "What is it that God wants of me?" Only by doing this can you strengthen your relationship with God and find meaning in the world. For that *is* the essential task for all of us, to strengthen that relationship.

Anyone who stops to think, truly think about the meaning of life, must come to a similar conclusion. There *must* be more. It just doesn't make sense that the ultimate purpose of life is nothing more than sated physical needs and satisfying base pleasures. The truth is, so much of life is suffering, pain, anxiety and frustration. As a teacher of mine once said, "I just can't believe that God placed me here on this earth for sixty or seventy years to eat a few hundred thousand chickens or hamburgers or hot dogs, drink a few thousand gallons of Coke or Pepsi, live it up and have a blast… and then die.

"There must be more!"

It is true. This vessel of ours, our body, must be more than just the sum of its parts – cells, tissues, organs. It must be a medium through which we can reach greater heights and accomplish more than just the satisfaction of base lusts.

We are *both* body and soul. One cannot help but affect and effect the other. Just as a "fire in the bosom" will burn the clothes, improper clothes will foul the inner person. One cannot exist properly without the other. Make no mistake, there can be no mismatch when it comes to piety. The outward appearance of piety without inner piety is, at best, hypocrisy. Inner piety without an outward manifestation of it – in acts and in appearance – is delusional.

Though it might come as a shock to those invested in the modern world, the issues of sin, piety and good works are not about quantity (although it comes as no surprise that people *want* to quantify these things. They want to quantify everything – which is the essence of living in the physical rather than the spiritual world.) They are *qualitative* issues and, as such, have not changed since the Garden of Eden. The face of our temptations might be new, we might drive large cars and live in houses whose luxury was unthinkable in the ancient world but even King David was seduced by his passions. Men, and women, have always been haughty, arrogant, and selfish. There is, sadly, nothing new in this. As Kohelet says, "There is nothing new under the sun."

This recognition does, however, teach us something. It teaches us that the striving to be closer to what God commands us to be implies that there will always be – and there has always been – a "falling short." We are human beings. We are not perfect. We can't be. At best, at our very best, we are individuals *striving* to conform to God's commands. Always moving toward; never, in this world, quite perfectly realizing our goal.

While religious teachers have often spoken about this inner aspect of our being, it is, in truth, highly subjective. For who among us can accurately meas-

ure the goodness in our own soul, let alone someone else's? So it is no surprise that there is a corresponding degree of subjectivity in defining the appropriate dress and behavior for the *bat Yehudit* – the pious Jewess.

Indeed, contrary to the modern notion that the more pious a person, the
more comfortably he or she incorporates piety, we are taught that the "striving" is actually harder for the more pious and, as our rabbis taught, "the
greater the man, the stronger his *yetzer rah.*" So it is no wonder that the more
pious the person, the more modestly he or she dresses. After all, effecting our
external appearance is the most direct and obvious way to affect our inner
selves and to gain the upper hand against our temptations.

It is a cruel irony that the more pious, the greater the temptation to "fall
short." Those who have greater potential and responsibility have a corre-
spondingly great temptation to overcome. Why should this be? Because our
lives are always in balanced tension. The greater the good, the greater the
corresponding temptation to do bad. Passion is not solely in the domain of
those who are invested in the physical. However, passion for God and goodness brings more meaning, more self-respect and a more fulfilling life than
the passion for the mere physical ever could.

The nexus of our physical selves and spiritual selves is our relationship
with someone of the opposite sex. How to best address the dynamic between
the sexes and how this dynamic relates to *tzniut*? I once knew a man who explained *tzniut* to his daughter by focusing on the "impulses" of boys. He made
it plain that the reason for *tzniut* was to keep his daughter from appearing or
behaving in such a way so as to draw the attention, and therefore engage the
"impulses" of boys.

This is not an uncommon explanation for *tzniut*. However, as consistent as
it is with the idea of "building a fence" around that which is pure to protect
it from that which is impure, I think it misses the fundamental point of *tzniut*
as having more to do with the inner-self than the outer-self.

What is most troubling to me about the notion that *tzniut* is essentially
about protecting women from the evil impulses of boys and men is that it
does exactly what our modern world does to women – it objectifies them and
categorizes them as sexual objects. True, the thrust of the modern world is to
be successful in turning women into sexual objects and the goal of this understanding of *tzniut* is to protect them from becoming sexual objects but in

both cases, that is the essential characterization of women – objectified in their sexuality.

Implicitly, the argument does the same to boys and men – reducing them to objects of impulsiveness and manipulation, objects whose sole goal is the degradation of girls and women; to be creatures (I use the term advisedly here!) who would take advantage of their first opportunity to take advantage of a girl or woman.

Without diminishing the power of sexual urges and without being blind to the dangers that such temptations pose, I still would argue against an understanding that objectifies either men or women. First, modern girls and women are hardly without resources. They are not helpless. Indeed, if women have ever been "helpless" it is only because a culture has rendered them such, the better to objectify them! But women have never been helpless. They are very capable of withstanding and turning away an inappropriate remark or gesture by a boorish male.

Secondarily, this explanation also calls into question the gift of beauty. For, despite the challenges we have alluded to above, beauty is still seen as a gift from God (remembering that beauty is in the eye of the beholder and modesty and virtue are essential elements of true beauty.) But perhaps the greatest concern I have with this reasoning is that it seems to contradict the Torah's approach to holiness, which is that we are each responsible for controlling our impulses. The ability, after all, is what distinguishes us from base animals.

Therefore, it is incumbent on the boy or man to control his impulses, not on the girl or woman to protect herself from it. After all, is it a Jewish idea that an individual should be limited in what he or she does because of *someone else's* inclination to commit a sin? The absurdity of that position should be self-evident. It certainly is in all other aspects of life. Why not in regards to our understanding of *tzniut*?

Shouldn't it bother us that this simplistic explanation goes against the idea of modesty in the body of Jewish law and tradition? One need only look back at the verse from Micah that we quoted above, "He has told thee, O man, what is good; and what does the Lord require of them, but to do justly, and to love true loyalty, and to walk humbly (*hatzanayah*) with thy God."

You will notice that in this seminal message from the prophet, there is no mention at all of men, of women, or of any conflict or relationship between the two. Its message is clear, to walk humbly (modestly) is to do so "with thy God."

Ultimately, we cannot discuss Jewish modesty without discussing human dignity. A modest person looks inside for his or her identity and then tries to find a way to have that inner self reflected in his or her outside self. What do you want people to "see" when they look at you? If you are a woman, do you want people to see your physical features or something more, something that goes to the essence of the good in you? If you are a man, do you want people to see your business acumen or your political power, the car you drive or something more important, your charity and determination to follow God's commands?

*Tzniut*, as it pertains to our physical presence, is a way to control the "message" we send out about ourselves. Our clothes and our personal items are our personal "bumper stickers" – communicating effective "sound bites" to those around us what we consider important, or vital to who we are, and who we hope to be.

When it comes to *tzniut* that message must be equally true whether anyone sees the message, whether we are behind closed doors in our own homes with our family, when we lie down and when we get up, or when we are on our way. In other words, it is a message that should be true to our innermost selves. It speaks directly to our striving, to our quest for our identity, our sense of self-worth, and personal dignity.

Of course, there is always One who can see us in our most private moments. And it is our relationship with that One that demands our attention. If we are striving for that good relationship with God then our sense of self worth and dignity simply *is*. There is no need to devise exercises to regain it or create it. We *know* we are worthy because the Creator has seen fit to imbue us with a soul.

This sense of self-worth and personal dignity has everything to do with the way man and woman should relate to one another. From the time that Adam and Eve walked in the Garden of Eden, the relationship between men and women has been a source of delight and spirituality, as well as a source of confusion and friction.

This duality does not diminish the need of each individual – man or woman – to engage in *tzniut* nor does it suggest that there is not equality between the sexes. It does acknowledge that men and woman are different and that it is equally wrong not to acknowledge and accept those differences as it is to treat either unfairly. This duality then, goes to the heart of why there are more laws governing *tzniut* and women then there are with men.

There *are* differences between the two sexes. Does that imply inequality? No. While "different" is clearly not "the same" it is also not necessarily unequal. Or unfair. More is expected of the pious than the sinner. Is there a difference between what is expected of the pious and the sinner? Yes. Is it unfair? No. Does it imply inequality? No. It acknowledges the very real difference between the two.

The wealthy have an obligation to give more than the poor. Is that unfair? Of course not. It is just.

The modern world has become enamored with the idea of equality as "sameness." Everyone should get the same pay, the same chance. Sameness is understood to be synonymous with equality. But they are not the same thing.

Different is different. One is not necessarily better or worse for the distinction.

Often in our modern world, we hear of women complaining that their domain in the house with the children diminishes them. They want to be out in the world, pursuing a profession, interacting with interesting people like their husbands who, toiling in the business world, presumably do extremely interesting things every day with the most interesting people imaginable.

We live at a time when physical beauty has come to equal worthiness. Mind you, this has always been a message in Western culture – and others as well. From fairy tales on, physical beauty has always been highly prized. After all, one cannot help but note that Cinderella was pretty while her wicked stepsisters were not. Still, for those who are familiar with the tale, I would argue that the real "ugliness" of the step-sisters had more to do with their meanness than their physical appearance, and Cinderella's beauty was more an expression of her sweetness and goodness.

Pretty features on someone with ugliness in their soul creates a harsh, haughty beauty – which is really no beauty at all. In other words, beauty has always had a prominent place in our culture but in the past it had been an expression of inner beauty, a metaphor. No longer! Now, it is Cinderella's physical beauty alone that makes her worthy of the Prince's attentions and even if her step-sisters had been kind their physical presence would have defined them as ugly.

We can disagree with this state of affairs but for now we must acknowledge that this is the reality that our wives and daughters, our sisters and mothers must confront every day. The question is, What are the very real effects of this sad state of affairs on people we care about?

One obvious effect is that of time. Men and women no longer age or mature at relatively equal rates. While a man can age into maturity, gaining experience and wisdom from his life's experiences and his study, a woman is expected to somehow "freeze" herself sometime in her twenties or thirties. Any sign of aging – whether gray hair, wrinkles, smile lines or, God forbid!, frown lines – is not merely an indication of the passing years and wisdom and experience gained but it is an indictment of her *diminishing* value as a human being!

Imagine! A woman who has given birth to children and has raised them, who has nurtured them, who has cared for her parents and her husband's parents, who has been a helpmate to her husband, who has borne the happiness and sadness of life… all of this is irrelevant! All that matters is that her body has changed; that she is too heavy (never too thin!); that her hair is gray; that her eyes have bags under them; that something, some aspect of her physical self, has begun to show the signs of time and experiences.

And how must this affect each individual woman? How can she look upon her family, which she has loved and cared for, the children she has nursed through fevers and illness, the way she has struggled to make ends meet when times where tough and think to herself, "What a fine job I've done!" No! She must instead think to herself, "What a fright I must look!" She cannot look at herself and say, "My arms are strong from carrying all my children." She must say instead, "How much more toned my arms would be if I was working out in the gym! That's what I *should* be doing!"

The judgments of our culture are no less cruel for young girls and women. These poor souls are not seen for their goodness and kindness, for the innocence with which they engage the world. They are not appreciated for the time they devote helping their mothers or their grandmothers, or the care they give their younger siblings. They do not receive adequate praise for the consideration and respect they show their elderly neighbors. No. Instead, they gaze upon themselves in the mirror and see their bodies alone. And, according to the relentless critique of our culture, there is nothing that they see that they can be happy or satisfied with.

Could any perspective be further from *tzniut?*

Where our culture has focused more and more on the surface, on the superficial, on the outermost aspect of who we are, Judaism insists on looking at the inside. When our culture cries out: Display yourself! For it is by your display that you are correctly judged! Judaism speaks firmly and delivers an opposing message: Protect your goodness. Build a fence around it. Let your outside be beautiful *because* it reflects your inner goodness.

It is as if you carried a light into a smoke-filled room. The smoke can only diminish the brightness of the light. So, you cover the light. You protect it. So that when it is necessary and when it is appropriate, the light will shine like a thousand watt bulb.

Before Adam and Eve were cast from the Garden, the physical and the spiritual were in perfect balance. But since then, there is a constant struggle between the physical and the spiritual. The soul wants to pray. The body longs for chocolate.

Whereas the body and soul once worked in union for the dignity and full spiritual and physical fulfillment of the individual, now they seem to work at cross purposes, determined to undermine the other.

*Tzniut,* while unable to completely mend that which was damaged, is a way to reestablish that balance. It is a discipline by which the body is brought into congruence with what is best in the soul. It is a discipline that will allow you to not be distracted by the demands, the illusions, and the objectifying nature of the physical. It is an attempt to make private the spiritual, and to take away the concept of being "on display" – in all its manifestations.

Jewish tradition holds that all true heroic acts are done in private, where only you and God truly know your heart. That is, no public declaration. No awards. No recognition. Just you and God. Is there any better definition of what it might mean to be modest?

In pursuit of this image of beauty, girls and women (and also, in many regards, boys and men!) go to great and sometimes damaging lengths. People go to gyms to make themselves "buff", they inject their flesh with products like Botox (which is a dangerous toxin), they have plastic surgery to alter their faces and their bodies. All in the pursuit of… what? An impossible ideal of beauty that is inappropriate to begin with. Along the way, many individuals suffer thousands of minor and major insults to their psyches and their bodies. Why? So plastic surgeons can become wealthy? So drug and cosmetic companies can earn obscene profits? So their own greedy desires can be fulfilled?

This question of "why" is essential to our understanding of *tzinut*. It is as important as the decision about "what?" – what to wear. For the sense of modesty that informs all of these decisions is an internal one first and foremost, one that is reflected in the way we appear to "the world."

There are those who wonder why they can't "do or wear whatever they want" in terms of how they look or dress. They might even note that to suggest that their dressing or looking a certain way does not make someone else think or behave inappropriately. That, they say, would be "blaming the victim." While it is true that "blaming the victim" has a long and sordid history, such a defense misses the point. People who suggest that they can do or wear "whatever they want" invariably define their sense of who they are in terms of acquisition and possession. Things "belong" to them. The clothes are "theirs," the house is "theirs." Everything is theirs. Including their bodies.

While their bodies certainly don't "belong" to anyone else, their sensibility is misguided. It would be wiser to think of their bodies as being "on loan" – temporary housing for their souls. Not unlike an apartment that is rented rather than a house that is "owned."

Maimonides, in the Mishneh Torah, says that the Torah teaches that no one has complete ownership of his or her body. Responsibility, yes. Ownership, no.

Our bodies are "loaned" to us from God for safekeeping. We must recognize that our bodies are on loan and that their ultimate value is in protecting and nurturing what resides inside – our souls. It is for the sake of our souls that we are obligated to take good care of our bodies. This would not only justify a healthy exercise routine but obligate us to engage in one. Why? How we treat our bodies is reflective of how we care for our souls.

If we respect our bodies, we are making a statement about how we respect our souls. And, if we respect our souls, we cannot help but respect our bodies.

But sadly, that is not how our culture thinks. On March 17, 2007, Judith Warner wrote a column entitled "Hot Tots, and Moms Hot to Trot." Underlying the numerous and disturbing assertions made in her column, Ms. Warner was of the contention that mothers of young girls are encouraging negative behaviors and body images through their own distorted sense of their bodies and their selves.

Ms. Warner decries "bling-bling Barbies" as part of a culture that betrays young girls and women. She notes that the American Psychological Association has issued a report on the dangers of the "sexualization" of girls. The sexualization of girls? What have we come to, that such a concern has to be formally articulated as a "danger" by such an august body? Shouldn't this be a given in the world; that young women – girls! – should not be "sexualized"? What madness has taken over our culture that it requires a formal report by the American Psychological Association to even begin to focus on this as a problem?

I fully respect and understand those who pause at the way in which religious conservatism has colored political discourse in the United States. I appreciate those whose understanding of science and technology gives them pause when considering the religious truths expounded by others. I share with them the horror in acknowledging the tragedies that "religion" has perpetrated upon millions of people in the history of the world. However, can anyone who seeks to distance the spiritual from the culture, who does not share in any "mainstream" faith – be it Jewish, Christian, Moslem or other – really say that the secular culture, which has brought us "bling-bling Barbies" has not failed to deliver a better world?

Ms. Warner tells us, unsurprisingly, that the report found that "…sexualization – turning someone into 'eye candy' – is linked to eating disorders, low self-esteem and depression in girls and women." We are astonished that anyone might find such a conclusion a surprise. How could it be any other way? And yet, Ms. Warner's real target is not the books, magazines, movies and music that reinforce this negative and destructive message to young girls.

Her real target is moms.

While she acknowledges that moms tend to "talk a good game on things like body image…" she is right on target to point out that there is no "walk" behind the talk. Moms, she suggests, "…walk around the house sucking…

their stomachs in when they pass by a mirror." They obsess about the contents of their refrigerators in the name of "purity" when, in fact, it is in the name of the ever-elusive goal of "never being too thin."

The good thing – and tragically, on another level, sad thing – is that their young daughters see right through this hypocrisy. According to the article, by the time these young girls are in the eighth grade, they "...pretty much give up on their mothers..."

This is what our culture has come to – fourteen-year old girls, embarrassed by their mothers sad and pathetic desire to be eighteen-years old again. This is what our culture has created.

It is damnable, true.

But convincing mothers and daughters that they were not merely sexual objects would only be part of the solution. And this is where a secular, cultural solution cannot help but fall short.

A desire on the parts of mothers to teach their daughters "good body image" can not succeed if it is only a function of fashion. In other words, if it is only another approach. It is only when it is tied in with the desire to achieve *kedusha* – holiness – that it can be transformative.

And that is what we are talking about, isn't it?

My read of Ms. Warner's article – and I have no reason to believe she is Jewish, let alone an Orthodox Jew – is that she believes that girls and young women would be a lot better off (as does the American Psychological Association) if their mothers would learn to love themselves.

Mothers, according to Ms. Warner, have allowed themselves to be objectified and seem to have bought into that system so thoroughly that they are participants in objectifying themselves – she refers to classes in pole dancing and strip teasing classes taught at sports clubs – that there is virtually no possibility that they could do anything *but* participate in the same process for their daughters.

The only solution is to break the cycle.

But how? By not being "augmented" themselves? Or by being the kinds of moms who, as Ms. Warner describes it, "strut their stuff in spaghetti straps and spandex?" By convincing their daughters *not* to wear similar apparel? What would they remove from their medicine chests? Face creams? Wrinkle removers? What "procedures" would they deny themselves? Botox? Tummy tucks? Breast implants? Facelifts? Nose jobs?

We live in a society where many girls receive for a Bat Mitzvah gift a nose job! They receive breast augmentation for their high school graduation!

What does this say about the status of our culture? What are we doing to our children? And most importantly, how do we break the cycle?

With better cosmetics?

With longer dresses?

With more lectures about "positive" body image?

With all due respect, I believe that these things will continue to miss the point because each of these "solutions" amount to little more than a different piece of driftwood floating in the same stream. It is the stream itself that needs to be changed.

For each of these possible reactions to what is nothing less than a crisis in how we are raising this next generation of young girls is little more than a comment on fashion. What is astounding is discovering that so many people continue to be astonished that these kinds of "solutions" will not work.

Why not? Because they only address the symptom, not the cause. They are "solutions" that are thought to be ends in and of themselves. They do not "lead to" something more, something more meaningful and important.

They do not represent a call to *kedusha*.

*Tzniut* is a posture, a statement, a positional dynamic that has *everything* to do with *kedusha*, with holiness. And it is only a commitment to holiness that can break the tragic dynamic that has gripped our times. If a person is more interested in the external rather than the internal – more concerned about how others see her rather than how God sees her – then whether she wears a long dress or a miniskirt is of little consequence. She is focused on fashion. She is worried about how she is viewed as an objectified, physical object. The size and shape of her nose, her breasts, her legs are all more important than her intrinsic goodness. But if her focus is on what's good and right in the eyes of God, then there will be no question that "bling-bling Barbies" will not be of tremendous concern.

There will be no need for another lecture on self-respect, or another work-shop on how to "teach" our children self-worth. Self-worth is the "default" feeling. It is the *natural* feeling that they would have if not for the forces in our culture that emphasize the outward rather than the inward. Self-worth and self-respect are gifts that God has given to them – and us.

The resulting problem then is not one of "body image". It is a problem of the soul. Which is the reason that we can say that *tzniut* is not about fashion. It is not a "cover up." We do not measure *tzniut* with a length of cloth. How a *tznuah* dresses is a reflection of her inner humility and modesty, not a statement of her conformance with the standards defined by fashion – in any place or time.

There is no one manner of dress that is correct for every place and time. Nor should there be. *Tzniut* is not a static position. It is not rigid. Quite the contrary. *Tzniut* is a dynamic, fluid perspective, not a static pose.

In short, modesty **_leads to_**; it is not an end in and of itself.

*Tzniut* leads to holiness. Holiness is within, where it can be hidden and protected. Nothing recommends this notion of "hiddenness" more eloquently than noting that it stands in diametric opposition to American culture. Read newspapers or magazines, view Internet blogs, and sites such as MySpace and it seems that no one cares *why* their names appear in these forums, whether for noble or ignoble behaviors, so long as their names appear.

The logic of "hiddenness" is clear. If modesty elevates and exposure trivializes and if we recognize that what is being elevated or trivialized is not the holy source that we stand in relation to but ourselves and the nature of that relationship, then modesty must necessarily be understood not just in the context of *kedusha* but also as a form of self-respect. Secular social workers and psychologists seem to feel that it is this very concept – self-respect – which is at the root of the self-image difficulties our children seem to struggle with.

But what is self-respect after all? In Judaism, it is rooted in dignity. According to traditional Judaism, while there is nothing wrong (and many things to admire) about possessing riches, there is equally nothing "wrong" with *not* having money. In Judaism, money and riches are not the "currency" of dignity. How unlike the modern cultural dynamic which elevates the acquisition of money and things above all else?

Dignity does not require a "shout out." It does not proclaim itself. It does not require "spin." It does not have press agents. Indeed, dignity thrives in obscurity. How many midrashic tales and Jewish folk tales have as a main character the beggar who, in reality, is a messenger of God? And, almost always, it is a child who recognizes the true nature of this "beggar".

What do these stories teach us? Obviously, they teach us a great many things. They graphically demonstrate that, in Jewish tradition, that which is vital is far removed from the surface, from that which is incessantly revealed. They also tell us that those with the eyes to recognize this truth are those who are "innocent", who haven't been inundated with the world's notion of what accounts for "worth."

Of course, in these stories, the beggar is never arrogant or mean. He is, in actuality, the perfect picture of humility. Through his example, we learn how one's honor and dignity increase through tzniut.

Curiously, with the image of the beggar as a reference point, we begin to see what the proud, haughty person really is. Unlike the beggar, whose dignity is the natural consequence of his inner strength and holiness, the haughty person has no meaningful inner self and so burdens himself with the encumbrances of wealth and honor. Of course, this wealth and honor is the wealth and honor that the world recognizes as such, not that God does. The haughty person would expect us to bow before his riches. His life is an open proclamation that, "I am somebody!"

If you doubt it, just ask him. He will repeat the assertion with ever greater insistence.

How sad it is for us when we discover that he is, in fact, a nobody. That such a haughty, proud person has no sense of self. He has no self-respect and no self-dignity. Because of the absence of these worthy qualities, he is constantly trying to put himself "on display", exposing himself in an effort to externally create what so obviously does not exist internally. How terribly sad it must be when that haughty person faces his own day of reckoning, when *he* must finally realize that for all his pretension he is nothing more than a hollow vessel. He has allowed "the wine" to go rancid. That which he has deemed worthy is, in truth, worthless. And that which he has called beautiful is, in reality, ugly.

The proud and the haughty have no claim to honor which is, ironically, why they demand that they be honored! This is their fundamental contradiction. Sadly for them, it is impossible to construct honor from the outside in. No palatial surroundings, no suits of gold can pave the way for self-dignity. Theirs is a fool's errand. Dignity and honor always come from the inside out – which is why true dignity must be so carefully protected and why it is so important to conceal the outward expressions of holiness.

The glory of the beggar is mirrored in creation itself. For there, the budding of life is always hidden. The sprouting of a seed is done underground, away from the inquiring eyes of the world. Creation is holy. Its work is private work.

Like the budding seed, the soul must also be nurtured and created in private. This is what modesty allows for. This is part of what *tzniut* is.

*Tzniut* stands opposed to the calls of the culture to proclaim that the external is everything. It says that it is the <u>innermost</u> part of you that most – and best – defines you. Of all the many facets of your being – your physical self, your emotional self, your intellectual self – it is the one that animates all that is good and precious about you.

The question is, once you have started to look at yourself (as if in a spiritual mirror!) and recognized this valuable worthiness of self, how do you learn to convey the message of *tzniut*, that the value of your innermost self is revealed by how you look and act, rather than the opposite.

*Tzniut* is all about knowing how and when to reveal your body, your abilities, and all the other aspects of who you are so that you do not hide the special parts of who you are and reveal the other but that you cloak the other so that, in doing so, the special part of you, your inner beauty is what is revealed.

*Tzniut* is a process by which you come to know yourself, that your identity – who you *really* are – is that innermost self. Curiously, while the "look" of the *tzanua* might be similar to the "look" of another, Judaism doesn't teach *tzniut* to erase individuality. That is not the purpose of *tzniut*, for you to be hidden to yourself and others. Quite the opposite. *Tzniut* is designed for you to find out who you <u>really</u> are, inside *and* outside. While the practice of *tzniut* involves modest dress, it does not require a woman's face or hands to be covered like other cultures that emphasize modest dress, notably Muslim culture. Why not? Wouldn't the logical extension of *tzniut* be to complete "cover up"? No. The face and hands define individuality. Just as no two sets of fingerprints are alike, no two faces are alike. If I were to show you photographs of the forearms, or even the legs, of thirty different women, would you be able to identify the ones belonging to a wife or a sister? If I showed the thirty different women the photographs of *their* own arms and legs, how many of them would be able to say, "That's me!"

Absent a very particular birthmark, no part of the body regularly covered by modest dress is particularly helpful in identifying who a person is. However, look at someone's face and you *know* who the person is. Listen to someone talk and *watch* the expression in their hands.

Our rabbis teach that for *each* of us the world was created. Each of us as an individual. With an individual identity and value and worth.

So, in the end, what can I conclude about what we say about *tzniut* while "standing on one foot"? It is clear that our society and culture puts our children at terrible risk by elevating the physical, emphasizing physical beauty and material possessions. As we have seen, this is a recipe for pain and suffering, for hurt, isolation and rejection.

So, on one foot… we have a soul of exceeding worth. Cloak the physical in order to allow the beauty of the soul to blossom. That is the beginning of genuine happiness and meaning.

It is the obligation of parents and grandparents, of grown-ups and teachers to protect our children from the cruelty of a world devoid of soul and meaning. Let us teach them that self-worth comes from within. Let us claim that self-worth for ourselves so that we do not *tell* them about *kedusha* but so that we model it in our own lives.

For an elaboration on this theme, see my:
**Sometimes You Are What You Wear! An Argument for Tzniut – Modesty** (www.modestybook.com) by Eliyahu Safran, Xlibris Corporation - 2007

# TO MOURN, TO REMEMBER

## A MEDITATION ON SAYING GOODBYE IN JEWISH TRADITION

young man is ushered into a private room by a troubled colleague. The young man, concerned about the colleague's uncomfortable manner, asks if everything is all right. She shakes her head and directs the young man toward a chair. When he has eased into the chair she looks at him and then, with watering eyes, glances away. She draws a slow breath.

"What's wrong?" he asks, leaning forward.

In a shaking voice that the colleague struggles to keep firm yet caring, he is informed that the office had received a phone call a short while earlier. His father has passed away some fifteen thousand miles away.

"I'm so sorry," the colleague whispers, tears coming to her eyes.

"No, thank you," the young man mumbles, for the briefest of moments, more aware of her discomfort of his own situation or feelings. He blinks. "I'd just like to be alone if that's all right."

"You're sure?"

"Yes."

She nods and silently leaves the room, pausing to look back only once, in time to see her young colleague's face contort in a mask of grief, making him appear anything but a young man.

The door closes behind her.

The young man feels himself engulfed in a complete whiteness. There is no form. No structure. No past and no future. There is no left or right. There are no landmarks. No sounds.

Nothing. Not even emptiness which is, after all, a kind of fullness of nothing. There is not even *that*.

Just unrelenting *nothing*.

And then these words come to his lips: *Baruch Dayan Haemet -*

*Blessed are You, the True Judge.*

He does not know from where in his formless consciousness these words have taken shape and come forth. Having been so fortunate for all of his twenty-five years to have never before had to confront the death of a loved one or even someone remotely close to him, his familiarity with death and dying has been distanced – more intellectual than emotional; more theoretical than spiritual.

*Blessed are You, the True Judge.*

In truth, he feels anger at those words. He hates them as soon as they have crossed his lips. He instantaneously rails against them. In the instant that the words have formed, the full contours of his grief have taken shape, along with the fullness of his loss. How can he bless God, at a moment like this? His father has died!

The question though, is not how he could bless God at such a painful moment. The question is, How could he not?

These words, words that Jewish tradition teach should be uttered when one hears of a death, *Blessed are You, the True Judge*, speak at once to our complete smallness in the face of death and to the greatness of God. They speak to our unutterable loss, to a pain that is only a foreshadowing of the pain and sadness to come. To a knowledge that exists before knowledge.

In that first, incandescent flame of grief, when existence itself is as white and unrelenting as the totality of the emptiness of the page before the fledgling writer, the first words begin the process of recreating order in what will be a world reconfigured. These words, so simple an acknowledgement, so difficult a truth, represent the first step in the process of Jewish mourning, the process of losing a world and then, in the context of self and community, recreating the world anew.

These words are as fundamental a statement of our enduring faith as is, *Shema Yisrael.*

One should not minimize the existential, spiritual, psychological and social aspects of this statement as the first, small step in a sacred process. Jewish tradition teaches that "if one destroys a single life, it is as if he had destroyed the entire world." The meaning of this statement is clear. The value of each and every human life is equal to the whole of creation! Is it any wonder that when a life is taken from us, by whatever means, the world that we inhabit is fundamentally changed? If we were without a process to work through our grief, we would find ourselves unable to recreate a recognizable and meaningful world.

Without the ability to mourn, we could not be fully Jews.

DEATH AND DYING –

All that lives must die. This has been true since Adam and Eve, in choosing to disobey God in the Garden of Eden traded their personal immortality for a communal immortality. Neither the fact of death, its inevitability or its profoundly uniformity of its application seem to protect us from our fear and trembling in the face of that fundamental unknown.

Too rarely, dying is an orderly process, in which it is the ultimate destination of a long, well-lived life. A life defined by ritual and meaning. Within this context, the rites and rituals associated with death and dying actually become the foundation upon which the process of mourning is begun.

Every stage of life is important and meaningful. Does not the prophet Joel tell us that,

*Your sons and daughters shall prophesy,*
*your old men shall dream dreams,*
*your young men shall see visions.*

Every stage of life is honored and respected. None more than the wisdom of age and the distinction of the aged. Even so, as Jews we do not pretend that our rituals or faith overcomes our fear of death. The prospect of death is as frightening to us as it is to any person who has ever drawn breath.

As a matter of rhetoric if not of faith we distinguish between God as the Righteous Judge who sets a limit to our days on earth and the actual "executioner", the *Malach HaMavet* – the Angel of Death. Our faith in God is that He is a loving God and, while He may test us with trials, He loves us too much to exact this final punishment on us. In truth, we look to God to ultimately destroy *Malach HaMavet*.

As Isaiah prophecies,
*He will destroy death forever,*
*My Lord god will wipe the tears away from all faces*
*and will put an end to the humiliations of His people*
*throughout all of the earth*
*for it is the Lord who has spoken.*

Until that time, however, we stand before God, measuring our days and our accomplishments against that inevitable end.

It is a truth that we are born alone and we die alone. Who can share these existential moments with us, when our very beings are most defined as individuals. And yet, in both cases, our aloneness is not long-lasting. At birth, we are welcomed into the world by attendants and become part of family and a community.

That same community provides for us in death. Upon our death, a *Hevrah Kadisha*, a "sacred society" takes charge of our body. With prayers and psalms, our body is ritually cleaned and prepared for burial. At no time from the time of death until burial is the body left alone.

Two realities define each and every aspect of the rituals of death. The first is God as Judge. The second is that the dignity of the deceased must be guarded. The lessons of Judaism teach that we are to protect the vulnerable – whether the widow, or the child. In this view, no one is ever *more* vulnerable than at death. Therefore, great care is taken to preserve the dignity of the dead.

Death imparts upon the deceased a ritual uncleanliness. Therefore, the *Hevrah Kadisha*, takes responsibility for ritually cleansing the body. After the body is washed and dried, it is dressed in the *kittel*, the shroud that is worn on Yom Kippur. The *tallis* is placed on the shoulders of the deceased. One of the four *tzitzit* is cut. For the dead are not subject to *mitzvot*.

The body is lowered into a plain coffin lined with a large shroud which will eventually cover the entire body.

Simplicity defines Jewish funerals. Every one of us is equal in death and the rituals and ceremonies reflect that.

### THE LIVING REMAIN – THE PURPOSE OF MOURNING

The rituals of death and burial guide the *process* of death. In the face of a great unknowing, rituals and sacred practices provide meaning. Although the initial response to death is profound grief, best symbolized by the renting of garments, even in that initial grief, as we have already seen, the first outlines of the *process of grieving* (rather than the experience of it) begins to take shape.

*Blessed are You, the True Judge.*

It is natural to feel profound loss when someone dies. All humans mourn this loss. Ritual mourning is a formalized path that we follow in order to give our loss meaning. As Jews, we seek meaning in all aspects of our lives. For us then, not just mourning but *ritual* mourning is a natural response to death.

Make no mistake, our loss is deep. Almost unimaginably so. Unspeakably so. Our world changes as a result of our loss; we mourn the death of the one we knew and loved because our world has been inextricably altered. Our psychological, emotional, and social landscape has been jolted. It is as if a terrible disaster – an earthquake or a hurricane – has stricken our internal landscape, changing the emotional ground beneath our feet.

We mourn not only the loss of the person who was a part of our lives up to the present but also in anticipation of the terrible absence in going forward. Death puts an end to human potential. All that our loved one could be, was. There are no more possibilities. No more dreams to dream.

What's more, we mourn more than the loss of our loved one. Each and every death reminds us of the frailty of man; there will always be dreams that will go undreamed, potential that will go unrealized.

Each and every death forces us to confront our own mortality.

The final accounting brought into stark relief by death demands that we see the fog of our daily lives and the incessant demands of the *now* and truly ponder the value and meaning of life. Death is a breach from which we cannot turn away.

If we mourn "well" then we will come away from our period of mourning with a greater sense of the precious opportunities that life affords us – in our personal relationships, in our involvement in the community, in our caring for others and our relationship with God. Our tradition teaches that it is beneficial to mourn. The Preacher, Kohelet, goes so far as to teach, "It is better to go to the house of mourning than to go to the house of feasting, for that is the end of all men and the living will lay it to his heart."

Indeed, to mourn is to fulfill a Divine commandment. "Whoever does not mourn in the manner prescribed by the rabbis is cruel."

In the face of such a profound loss as the death of a loved one, how could we not mourn? In the face of death, we stand incomplete, and confused; our lives have been confused. The basic assumptions we have made seem to have been upended. In death, we witness the polar opposite of life, of God and of man. It is inconceivable that in such dire circumstance we would simply go on as before.

Death is transformative to everyone.

But the nature of the transformation is in limbo. The mourner finds himself devitalized, depersonalized, and de-identified in his normal relationships to family, friends and community.

On one level, mourning is a confrontation with a "diminished form of human existence." Human dignity has been stripped. The divine image in man has been degraded. It is painful. It is unbearable. It forces each of us to confront without filter the limits of man and the underachievement inherent in our natures.

The mourner often experiences guilt. Might he have done more? Might he have shared more? Might he have reached out a caring hand *just one more time*? Thomas Carlyle, the Scottish essayist, satirist and historian was going through his wife's papers after her death. Amongst the many papers, he found note after note reflecting her deep love for him and a yearning that he would give of himself to her in a larger measure. Reading those notes, he cried out in anguish, "If I had only known! If I had only known!"

If we had only known.

In *Tom Brown's School Days*, the hero of the story is on a fishing trip when he learns of the death of his schoolmaster. He returns immediately, and once back at the school sits alone in the chapel, where his teacher had been buried under the altar. Turning to the pulpit and leaning forward with his head in his hands.

*If he could only have seen the doctor again for five minutes; have told him all that was in his heart, what he owed to him, how he loved and revered him, and would by God's help follow his steps in life and death, he could have borne it all without a murmur. But that he should have gone away forever without knowing it at all, was too much to bear.*

Too much to bear indeed.

How often does the mourner beat his breast, wishing that he could have said more, done more, been more. George Eliot writes,

*Oh the anguish of the thought, that we can never atone to our dead for the stinted affection we gave them, for the little reverence we showed to that sacred human soul that lived so close to us, and was the divinest thing God had given us to know.*

This state of self-negation, resignation, self-doubt and despair in the face of death forms the Halakhic state of mourning. The one who has been touched by anti-life sits in rent garments, on the ground, without shoes, unkempt, unwashed, engaged in neither work nor the study of Torah. He is exempt from the recital of the Shema and from prayer and from *tefillin* and from all precepts laid down in the Torah.

The mourner does not recite the benedictions before or after meals; he may not repeat the "amen" when he hears the benedictions. In the face of death, man's relationships are temporarily suspended, even with God. Coming face to face with death precludes any normal activity or even divinely ordained obligations.

*Our commitment to God is rooted in our awareness of human dignity,* tzelem Elohim, *and sanctity. Once the perplexed, despairing individual begins to question whether or not such distinctiveness or special-ness exists, the sole commitment is suspended. Man who has faith in himself, who is aware of his human charisma, was chosen to carry obligations and commandments. Despairing, skeptical, denying man was not so selected. How can man pray and address God if he doubts his very humanity, if speech is stripped by his doubts of its human characteristics and turned into mere physical sounds? How can the mourner pronounce a benediction or say 'amen' if he is speechless?*

Death, by its very nature, forces us to doubt whether, in the whole of creation, we are somehow special. It creates in us the feeling that we are tumbling from grace. We are lost. The very thing that had always given us succor, our deep knowledge in our dignity because we are created in God's image, is lost.

For how can we be in God's image when God is, first and foremost, beyond the bounds of life and death and we, His creatures, are so painfully aware of our entrapment in time and in death?

Death makes us acutely aware of our smallness and, save but for God's grace, our insignificance. Yet, the process of mourning teaches us that we cannot, nor were we meant, to remain mired in a diminished form of existence. Grief, that nearly unbearable immediacy of loss, cannot, by definition, continue to define our response to loss. Nor should it. There is no experience within the realm of Jewish behavior and tradition which has as its sole purpose and goal the self-deprecation and denial of human dignity.

Judaism holds that man is not only free but is also master over his own deeds and emotions. Even during those times when self-denial is sanctioned, as during Yom Kippur, there is always a higher goal. During Yom Kippur, it is the *teshuva* (literally, 'return' but with the force of 'repentance' and 'transformation' here) realized by the process of anarchically prescribed self-denial.

What is the 'higher goal' we can achieve by mourning?

In the paragraph quoted above, in which the Rambam opens with the declaration that, "whoever does not mourn the dead in the manner prescribed by the rabbis is cruel" he anticipates our need to understand exactly how this 'cruelty' can be averted. Certainly, when we examine the *actions* of mourning, the renting of garments, not shaving or washing, not wearing shoes, sitting on the ground, etc. we must conclude that it cannot be these actions alone which have the potential to raise us up.

Those who misunderstand the power of Judaism and the mysterious faith which has animated our people for millennia point to such proscribed actions and conclude that Judaism is a 'legalistic' religion, one devoted to following the 'letter of the law' at the expense of the 'spirit of the law'.

How wrong they are!

If behavior alone was sufficient to attain the higher goal of mourning then the words of Rambam would not make sense. Reading Rambam, one comes away with the sense that his thesis is to make clear that one is cruel if the confrontational state of fear, trepidation, and silence involved with mourning is not translated into the state of *teshuvah*. In other words, if the actions of mourning do not result in transformation, then the mourning process has indeed been 'cruel'.

*Rather, one should be apprehensive, troubled, investigate his conduct, and return in repentance. If one of the company dies, all the members thereof should be troubled. During the first three days the mourner should think of himself as if a sword is resting upon his neck, from the third to the seventh day as if it was lying in the corner, thereafter as if it moving toward him in the street.*

Perhaps Rambam's intent is to be instructive of how the mourner is not to remain cruel to himself. Certainly, to remain in a state of grief, or 'new mourning' – when it is as if a sword rests upon one's neck – would be cruel.

The lesson of Judaism is clear. Death is inevitable. Life is good. Thus we can echo the words of Job when he declared, "God gave, and God has taken. Blessed be the name of God."

The denial of death is, ultimately, the denial of life. What other faith or creed sees the sanctity of life overflowing into the acceptance of death; that sees both life and death as coming from the same source and therefore, both as blessed?

Life *and* death are to be understood in this context. This is the first, difficult task of the mourner, to be able to echo in his heart the words of Job, "God gave, and God has taken. Blessed be the name of God."

After the initial shock of death, after the first, fiery flame of grief, there begins the process of *avelut*, whose goal is to return and transform (*teshuvah*) the one confronted with anti-life into the full awareness of the blessings of life.

The process is *avelut*. The goal is *teshuvah*.

Rambam teaches that in order to avoid cruelty, "one should return in repentance." With the goal of repentance, transformation in the face of this existential crisis is not only possible, but desirable. In his writing, Rambam does not diminish the difficulty of the mourner. He plots out the process, the ascendancy, of mourning in the most dire terms. Even after the first moments of intense grief and through the funeral, the "way back" is not an easy one. For the first three days (of the *shiva* period), he writes that a sword is resting upon the mourner's neck. While, for the latter four days, it is as if the sword has been moved to the corner of the room and during the thirty-day period of mourning (*shlosim*) it is as if it is in the marketplace.

How can we parse Rambam's allegory here so that it best helps us understand what it means to mourn? One may ask why, in light of the pain and sorrow the mourner already feels, Rambam sees the need to add this dark image of the sword hanging first over their heads and then further and further away? While it is clear that the mourner requires a period of adjustment after the death of a loved one; but why this?

We choose to read Rambam here not as though he were 'adding' to the burden of the mourner but rather in the descriptive mode. He is plotting out *what* the mourner is actually experiencing in the earliest days and weeks after the loss of a loved one.

Who among us has not entered a house of mourning and felt his 'heart in his throat'? Who has not experienced that physical sensation that accompanies a fear and trembling similar to what Kierkegaarde wrote about, a fear and trembling in the face of a vast unknowing?

How much more so is that in the mourner's experience!

During those first three days of *shiva*, when grief is so sharp, so immediate, so painful that the mourner might forget to eat, to sleep, to do anything according to what had been the normal rhythm of his life, it is not unreasonable to liken the experience to having a 'sword against your neck'. Death is that close. That immediate. That real. However, as the days and hours slowly move forward, that is, as *life* continues, even the mourner begins to be drawn back into the normal rhythms of life. The *immediacy* of the confrontation with death is reduced – not by much, but a little. And in this subtle change, the mourner begins to become more conscious of the living and to the community. His attention is beginning, already, to shift.

The sword rests not against the mourner's neck but rather in the corner of the room. Rambam's sword no longer hangs directly over the mourner's head but it is slightly removed. Finally, as the mourner leaves the *shiva* period and enters the period of *shloshim*, when he begins to engage in the reality of the everyday again, Rambam's sword is even further removed. The mourner continues to 'feel' the reality of the sword even in the marketplace, the place of commerce and community. Yes, the sense of loss remains real and immediate and yes, the voice is ever-present but these realities are now intermingling with the reality of the everyday, with the community and with commerce. The mourner is beginning to reenter the everyday world of time and experience.

Even understanding Rambam in this way, one could still ask why he required these additional sharpened and focused descriptives of the tragic reality of ultimate loss. Certainly, they are not necessary to help a mourner confront that "diminished form of human existence" that results from such a profound loss.

*Reflections of this nature will put him on his mettle, he will bestir himself and repent, for it is written: "You have stricken them but they were not affected." (Jer. (5:3)*
*He should therefore be wide awake and deeply moved.*

So then, *teshuvah* is the reason. Transformation. In this understanding, mourning a loved one who has died becomes consistent with the Yom Kippur *teshuvah* experience. Many of the same prohibitions and restrictions apply to both. If the actions of both are similar then it seems not to be unreasonable that the goals of both are similar as well.

As we have seen, the restrictions of Yom Kippur are meant to 'afflict the soul' but for a very powerful and positive purpose – *teshuvah*. Transformation. That the 'affliction' might cause the 'afflicted' to become a better person. That the 'affliction' might cause the 'afflicted' to repent.

By depriving oneself of basic physical needs and pleasures on Yom Kippur, the Jew comes to recognize his frailties, his shortcomings, iniquities and failings. In other words, he comes face to face with the *self* that must be improved upon, which must move closer to God, which must repent. The essence of the Yom Kippur liturgy and experience is to bring the worshipper, through quiet and personal introspection, reflection, self-analysis and confession, closer to God.

In the same way, the mourner is cut off from the outside world of daily activity, removed from the pleasures and daily routine that has formed the basic rhythm of his life. He is limited in his social and religious interactions. He is, in short, left – if only by default – to look inward. He is confronted with his own quiet introspection and reflection. He must look directly at himself and his world in the context of his profound loss. And, in the context of that loss, evaluate the meaning and value of his life and behavior.

In short, so that he will perform *teshuvah*. In Rambam's words, *Kol zeh, lehachin atzmo veyachzor veyahur mishenato* [So that he will bestir himself and repent.]

As the *Sefer Hahinuch* reaches the same conclusion with remarkable clarity. *Therefore, when he suffers the blow of the occurrence of death for one of his near kin, for whom nature makes affection inevitable, the Torah obligates him to do certain things himself which will move him to focus his thought on the grief that has come to him. Then he will know and understand in his soul that his sins have caused him to be visited with this grief... Then as a man ponders this theme in his heart during the activity of mourning, he will set his mind to achieve repentance and will make his deeds worthy according to his ability.*

## YOM KIPPUR – YIZKOR

It is due to the common bond that exists between mourning and repentance that we come to understand why the memorial prayer service for the dead – *yizkor* – was originally recited only on Yom Kippur and not during all three of the *shalosh regalim*. And indeed, the theme of Yom Kippur is, in fact, the theme of the entire *yamim hanoraim* season. We pray fervently for life. "Remember us unto life, O King, who desirest life."

"Our Father, our King, inscribe us in the Book of Life."

It seems at first glance to be incongruous that we would 'interrupt' this intense focus on life to shift our attention to our memories of those who are no longer amongst the living and to recite the *yizkor* liturgy for the departed. The explanation for this seeming paradox is that, of course, that there is no paradox at all. Jewish tradition views life as continuous from generation to generation. *L'dor vador*. Jewish tradition is a golden chain with each link represented by a generation. A powerful commonality unites the living with the dead. The confessional prayers, *vidui*, are stated not merely as reflective of our own deeds, but as our fathers' as well. "For we are not so brazen and obstinate as to say before you, Hashem, our God and God of our forefathers, that we are righteous and have not sinned – rather, we and our forefathers sinned." The *Kohein Gadol*, too, beseeched God for forgiveness in the name of "Your people, the family of Israel.

All Israel.

For all time.

*Yizkor* is a time of communication; an occasion when the departed souls join with and speak to us and with us, reminding us of hopes and dreams which were theirs and which are now ours. Given this understanding, what more appropriate day is there to rejoin with the souls of the departed than on Yom Kippur?

Enlarging on the lessons of the individual mourner, *yizkor* reminds us that man's pilgrimage on earth is limited. But more than individual man, a generation is limited, existing only as a link between yesterday and tomorrow. As individuals and as a community could we confront a more compelling reason to repent? Our days are numbered as were the days of our forebears. None of us ever finishes his work. As Rabbi Tarfon taught, "the day is long and the labor is mighty. It is not yours to complete the task..."

We are each, as individuals and as a community, given the task of completing the tasks of the generations before us, just as the generations to come will carry on where we have fallen short. How can we not respond to this reality with a determination to, at the least, do more? How can we not repent?

On Yom Kippur, when we reflect on and pray for a life of purpose and meaning, *yizkor* reminds us of the true meaning and purpose of our lives. It demands of us that we become a stronger link in the chain of tradition; that we renew our dedication to completing the work of those who came before us, and to lightening the load of those who will come after us.

The only genuine and authentic method of reciting *yizkor* is to be able to translate memories, emotions, and love of the past into new realities. To create transformation. Genuine tears, memories, and emotions are an unspoken acknowledgement that the present, that *we*, exist only by virtue of the past. That life without the lives of those who came before us is both meaningless and impossible. So too must the future rest upon us.

How full of awe must we be to see that truth clearly! How powerfully must we feel the weight of the past – of our personal past and our communal past. How mighty were those small acts of heroism and courage; how callous the world; and how much more had been left for our forebears to accomplish.

We can feel their touch once again. Hear their voices. Smell their smells.

Are we not then mourners? Is our experience, when experienced genuinely, not the experience of a mourner grieving anew? And so too, is not the mourner not confronting these same realities in his moment of grief? Does he not, in his grief, recognize that the death of his loved one is also a call for him to live; to repent and to transform his life?

Mourning those who came before us, with their love and dedication, must include a confession that our present is not only their past but also holds the seeds of the future yet to come. This awareness of the past as the foundation to our present and the key to the future is essential to *yizkor*. This is the way in which God has ordained life; that we never finish our work and it is therefore left for those who come after us to complete it. *Yizkor* calls us to hold high the ideals of the generations of Jews that have preceded ours, to cherish their dreams and aspirations, to share in their tears and heartaches.

They had set many goals for themselves – some simple, others lofty – which they did not realize. They were removed from the land of the living before fulfilling their potential. Now that we recognize and confront that loss and interruption, it is for us to continue.

*Your sons and daughters shall prophesy,*
*your old men shall dream dreams,*
*your young men shall see visions.*

KADDISH –

Repentance and transformation is not easy. First, it requires that we recognize that *what was* is irredeemably lost. This is painful. It is grieving at its most bare. We recognize what must be done and yet our pain is too great. We see the land ahead, but we cannot seem to make our feet march toward it.

When we recognize the need and obligation to continue and complete the unfinished tasks of those who came before us, we find that our pain is increased rather than lessened. We grieve rather than feel comforted. How can one go forward without the guidance of the past? How can the child move on but with the gentle and firm guidance of the parent?

How can we bridge the past to the future without the wisdom of our teachers, without the trust of our friend? Certainly the responsibility is too great and our sadness too deep. How can we now face up to the great challenge of our ancestors who "have left room for us to achieve and to distinguish ourselves?" As the days of mourning progress, our sadness accrues rather than lessens. We feel lonely. Life seems to have no meaning. How could it, without our loved one?

"How can I go on?" the mourner cries out. "From where will my help come?"

The answer, the only genuine answer is, "My help comes from God, Maker of heaven and earth." To empower the mourner, the one who has just stared into the terrifying grave and the end of man, the mourner is now re-invited to reestablish his relationship with God by reciting Kaddish again and again for the duration of the formal mourning period.

How is this reaffirmation of one's full faith in God to be accomplished however, particular through the recitation of a prayer that makes no mention of death or guilt or memory of the past. For the Kaddish is none of these things. Rather it is,

> *...a declaration of faith in Israel's national purpose, of loyalty to Israel's creator, or confidence in the ultimate triumph of the ideals for which heavens and earth were created, of longing for the time when people – all people – will accept the heavenly mission that gives meaning to life and transcends death, that will illuminate the darkest moments of personal and universal tragedy. Such an expression gives hope and direction to life and striving.*

Kaddish is, quite simply, a proclamation of faith. It is an <u>acceptance</u> of suffering, reflecting Divine purpose and judgment even in the face of death. It is Jewish tradition's answer to Dostoyevski's observation that, "without God murder would be but the falling of a leaf in the forest." It is God who gives meaning. Our acceptance of God's purpose and judgment renders death not completely 'the other' but promises that the death of our loved one is not for naught.

But Kaddish is not 'magic'. It does not erase the very human feelings and suffering that the mourner wrestles with. Quite the opposite. Kaddish *affirms* that the pain of the mourner is not a myth, it is real and meaningful. It is, in fact, the most difficult test of our faith.

Kaddish is a petition to God for relief. But it is not a standard *bakashah*, request. Rather, it is a painful recognition that our only hope for survival, for meaning, rests in the revelation on earth of the Divine presence. It is a higher form of prayer, in which our focus is not on our everyday needs and welfare but rather our focus is on our desire that the great name of God be sanctified. *Yehei sh'meih raba mevorakh.* Finally, through Kaddish, man resolves to dedicate himself to the goal of *Kiddush Hashem*, of bringing about the sanctification of God's name on earth, which may very well be considered the ultimate goal of repentance.

We see now that the recitation of the Kaddish, which sought God's help in sanctifying His name has become an instrument in the achieving this goal. For when we publicly proclaim our faith and prayer for God, we cause the entire congregation to respond to our words and to proclaim in a communal, unified voice, "*Amen. Yehei sheih rabba mevorakh l'alam ul'almei al'mayya.* May His great name be blessed from now until eternity!" It is this sanctification of God's name by the entire congregation, brought about by our recitation, that is the high point of the Kaddish.

The Rav casts this reality in its most dramatic terms. "The Kaddish," he says, "marks the beginning of a new phase of courageous and heroic mourning with a message of Divine salvation. When a mourner recites, '*yitgadal v'y-itkadash shmei rabba....*' He decleares that we are not giving up, that we are not surrendering, that we will carry on the work of our ancestors, that we will not be satisfied with less that the full realization of the ultimate resurrection of the dead, and eternal life for man."

*Teshuvah.*

The Kaddish then, is the 'voice' that speaks to the mourner, telling him that he is not alone in his loss. His loss is our loss. His loss is God's loss and therefore His name must be restored and magnified to its previous greatness. The loss of one individual, one Adam, is tragic not only for his loved ones but also for his Father in Heaven. Therefore, we need to console God by declaring that we who are left behind commit ourselves to help magnify and sanctify 'Your name.' The mourner, in reciting Kaddish, switches roles from one being consoled to becoming a consoler.

Kaddish moves the mourner as *yizkor* does, to raise his eyes and to see beyond the grave's mound. The days of our years in this world are numbered, our tasks go incomplete, our mission destined to be unfulfilled. This world's sojourn however is but a *prozdor* to the world of truth, the world of souls where the "righteous sit with their crowns on their heads and bask in the glory of God."

Kaddish reminds us, as does *yizkor*, that we should hold high the ideals of the past so that we can ensure a better and more secure future, that we should cherish the unfulfilled dreams and yet realize their aspirations, for after all, all Jews share in common dreams and will likewise share in their eventual realization. The passing of yesterday's Jew shifts the onus of responsibility to tomorrow's Jew in fulfilling the dream, even the ultimate dream, the messianic dream.

Our worth and meaning in this world is relevant because of the past, but more so because of the future.

The ultimate message of Kaddish is that man is not alone. And, saved from aloneness, even the tragedy of death can be given meaning.

Man is not alone. His worth is measured not simply by individual achievement but in the context of his community; by his interrelationship and connection to national dreams and aspirations, which can never be realized during the lifetime of any one individual. Thus, when the death of an individual is confronted, Kaddish reminds the mourner of the unbroken link with the only One who transcends mortality and assures immortality through the entirety and fulfillment of our collective dream throughout all the generations. And so the Kaddish concludes with the hope that ultimately, "May there be abundant peace from Heaven, and life, upon us, and upon all Israel."

### RESPONSE TO NATIONAL TRAGEDY –

It is clear that mourning is a personal journey. Even a communal one. As individuals, we grieve and mourn. As communities, we grieve and mourn. But what is the Jew's response to a national tragedy? What do we do when national dreams are shattered, collective goals destroyed and universal Jewish aspirations quashed. We have come to understand – and even appreciate – how to respond to an individual's *Churban.* How do we react to a national *Churban?*

How do we, as a people, react to a calamity so great that it brings our concept of peoplehood to its knees? How do we react, for example, to the destruction of our sacred Temples in Jerusalem?

Our First Temple, the *Beit Hamikdash,* built to replace the Tabernacle by Solomon in the 10th century BCE stood for four hundred and ten years. It was destroyed by the Babylonians under Nebuchadnezzar in 586 BCE as a result of our sinfulness. At the time, the people engaged in idolatry, forbidden relationships, and murder. With the destruction of the First Temple, we were taken into captivity in Babylonia. We wept and mourned our loss at that time.

As David wrote in Psalm 137:

By the waters of Babylon we sat down and wept, when we remembered Zion.

As for our lyres, we hung them up on the willows that grow in that land. For there our captors asked for a song, our tormentors called for mirth: 'Sing us one of the songs of Zion.'

How shall we sing the Lord's song in a strange land?

If I forget you, O Jerusalem, let my right hand forget its skill. Let my tongue cleave to the roof of my mouth if I do not remember you,

If I set not Jerusalem above my highest joy. Remember, O Lord, against the people of Edom the day of Jerusalem, how they said, 'Down with it, down with it, even to the ground.'

O daughter of Babylon, doomed to destruction, happy the one who repays you for all you have done to us; Who takes your little ones, and dashes them against the rock.

How we grieved and mourned. And then Cyrus of Persia led his people in battle against the Babylonians. When he defeated them, he allowed us to return to Jerusalem to rebuild the *Beit Hamikdash.*

In 70 CE the Second Temple was destroyed by soldiers of the Roman Empire led by General Titus. From that time forward, we wandered through the centuries, cast adrift from the land that God had promised us. The destruction of our Second Temple was a tragic story of the downfall of a nation, our nation. We, a once proud and noble people, reduced to a nation of wanderers, beggars and slaves, of a people once admired and revered, who became the object of scorn.

How far had the Lord's chosen fallen!

How could we possibly mourn such a national calamity in a way that brings about *teshuvah*? The destruction of the Second Temple changed the course of Jewish history and destiny. The subsequent changes wrought havoc and confusion to the religious, national, social and cultural context of the Jewish people. What comfort could there be found for a people when their "Holy city and the suburbs have become a disgrace and been looted, all her treasures have been buried and hidden? How could a broken people rekindle their faith "when I see every city built on its hilltop, while the City of God is degraded to the nethermost depth?"

Where is the comfort?

"I am that man who has seen affliction by the rod of His anger. He has driven me on and on into unrelieved darkness. Only against me did He turn His hand repeatedly all day long?"

Is *teshuvah* possible?

How can a people transform themselves in the face of such a calamity?

There are three kinds of responses to the destruction of the Temple, each directed at three different phases and serving different purposes relevant to the *Churban*. Each of the responses relates to specific elements of the *Churban*: past, future, and God. *Avelut* and tzaar – mourning – is a response to the past; *zikhronot, tziyunim,* and *semalim* – memorials and remembrances – focus on the future; *teshuvah* and introspection focus on our relationship with God.

The obligation to mourn and grieve over the destruction of Jerusalem and the Temple comes from the prophet Isaiah: "Rejoice with Jerusalem, and be glad with her, all you that love her; Rejoice for joy with her, all you that mourn for her."

On the basis of this verse, the Talmud teaches that "whoever mourns over Jerusalem merits to see her joy, and whoever does not mourn over Jerusalem does not see her joy." When 17th Tammuz heralds the advent of the Three Weeks of mourning, our remembrance of the destruction of God's dwelling place on earth culminates once again in the soul-searing tones of *Tisha B'Av's* mournful lamentations. The pain and sorrow we experience during this period, the restraints we practice, culminating in the actual mourning on the Ninth of Av, reawakens but a glimmer of recollection for the historic tragedy which forms the backdrop for our customs of mourning. There are those for whom the destruction forms the blueprint for their liturgical year. They are *Avelei Tzion*, Mourners of Zion. For them, the destruction of the Second Temple is an on-going tragedy. Since that time, the pious did not eat meat nor did they drink wine. When Rebbi Yehoshua questioned their practice, the pious responded, "Shall we eat meat that is offered on the *mizbeach* and is no more? Shall we drink wine that is sanctified on the *mizbeach* and is now dissolved?"

The pious asked, How can we go forward *as we did before*? How can we *not* be transformed and have our transformation reflected in our behavior?

The second form of *zikaron* obligation deriving from the *Churban* has two aspects. The first asks of us <u>active</u> remembrance of the destruction: leaving a spot of the house unpainted; leaving over a part of one's meal; making mention of Jerusalem in *tefillah* and *birkat hamazon*. In other words, we demonstrate a lacking in a direct, concrete manner. We come to this demonstration of our remembering from the verse in *Tehillim*: "If I forget thee, O Jerusalem, Let my right hand forget her cunning. Let my tongue cleave to the roof of my mouth; If I remember thee not: If I set not Jerusalem above my chiefest joy."

The well-known wedding custom of breaking a glass under the *chuppah* is likewise derived from mournful cry of the Psalmist.

These are all physical, concrete means of demonstrating that we will not forget that terrible tragedy; that the *actual* tragedy remains as real to us as it was to the poor souls whose eyes bore witness to those terrible days in the First Century C.E.

The second aspect of our obligation to remember Jerusalem and all that she represents Jewishly and halakhically comes from our performance of *mitzvot* just as they were enacted and performed in the *Mikdash* itself. For this reason, Reb Yochanan ben Zakai legislated that the *lulav* must be taken throughout for seven days as a *zekher l'Mikdash*.

The Talmud asks, "How do we know that we are to establish a remembrance for the *Mikdash*?" Reb Yochanan responds, because the verse says, "For I will restore health unto thee, and I will heal thee of thy wounds, says the Lord; because they have called thee an outcast: She is Zion, there is none that cares for her." The last part of the *Posuk Tzion hee doresh ein lah* teaches us that we are to seek Jerusalem out in the very manner which ideal Jerusalem exists. That is, *mitzvot*.

Beyond the obligation to perform *mitzvot* in the post-*Churban* times in the same manner in which they were performed in the *Mikdash* (in order to always make real and immediate the *Mikdash* experience), there is also an injunction to perform the *mitzvot* that were only performed in *Eretz Yisrael* during Temple days, outside *Eretz Yisrael* as well. Jeremiah exclaims: "Set thee up marks (*tziyunim*), make thee guide posts (*tamrurim*)" – markings and posts that will remind us of the paths we left behind in the land of Israel. (And which, therefore, mark the way *back*.) For by separating *terumot* and *ma'aserot* even out in your own land, we remember how to live in the land.

Chazal established three types of remembrances (*zikaron*) to help us to cope with the *Churban* experience. The first are *zikaron* experiences meant to invoke memories of Jerusalem throughout all of life's experiences, from the mundane, such as eating, or religious obligations, such as praying, and even at the most joyous times of our lives, such as marriage. With the Temple's destruction, there ascended a perpetual state of mourning upon the Jew's life experience.

We would never be the same.

We *should* never be the same.

If our remembrance of Jerusalem diminished, we would be diminished as a nation, as a people. Our past is not mere prelude to our present and future. It is an essential ingredient in who we are. We cannot be transformed without remaining in some very profound way unchanged. Therefore, though we could no longer offer sacrifices at the Temple, we offer prayers as both remembrance *and* as sacrifice. As memory and as action.

In very real ways, we internalize as a people the reality of the Temple so that our character and our actions as a nation continue to represent the reality of the Temple. We keep the Temple alive so that it remains a *living, dynamic* presence in our continued lives and so, when the Temple is rebuilt, we can return to it and reestablish the sacred rituals of the Temple *as if they had never been interrupted.*

Because of this, even the *choson* walks down the path of happiness with ashes on his own head, because even as an individual Jew, he is a member of the collective Jewish nation and for the collective Jew there can be no moment of joy, no unadulterated joy, without its memory of sadness, no experience in this life that does not connect to the Temple.

How many times have we heard a friend or family member say, while attending a *simcha*, "so-and-so would have loved to be here"? The absence of that loved one dampens the pure joy of the *simcha*. If an individual's absence can do that, how much more so is our joy moderated by the knowledge that the *Beit Mikdash* no longer stands in Jerusalem?

There are *zikaron* experiences that call to mind the lost regal *mitzvah* moments of the Temple; the great pageantry of the *Beit Mikdash*. Finally, there are remembrances of a total life style and religious-national mood that is no longer part of our Jewish routine. Each of these *zichronot* evoke emotions and sentiments of the world that was and which is sadly no more.

Just as active manifestations of mourning are insufficient for the individual mourner, so too are they lacking for the national response to the collec-

tive sense of mourning. Actions are not enough to honor our loss and to satisfy our emotions. It is not enough to light the *yarzheit* candle. Without something *more* it is merely an act, no different than lighting a candle in the evening
to ward of the darkness of the coming night.

The *Churban* demands more from our collective mourning, more than mere
memory. We have become a nation without *Kohanim* at our service, Levites at
our songs. We can no longer make our way to Jerusalem to satisfy the re-
quirements of the Three Pilgrimages. We are no longer able to offer up sacrifices to God.

No more does our Sanhedrin sit in authoritative judgment of the people,
determining what is right and wrong according to Torah.

We have lost so much of our spiritual vitality. We are left with quiet introspection and reflective thoughts. Fast days and commemorations. And so
we incorporate *zecher l'Mikdash* rituals, restrictions, lamentations and fasting.
But are they *necessary*? Does the "city and its inhabitants who sit in solitude,
who became like a widow, who weeps bitterly in the night and her tear is on
her cheek" need further prodding? Isn't our sadness and pain sufficient?
Aren't the constant reminders of our forlorn state enough to assure that, "If
I forget thee, O Jerusalem, let my right hand forget its cunning?"

> *There are days which are observed by all Israel as fasts because tragic events hap-*
> *pened on them, the object being to stir hearts and open the way to repentance, and*
> *to remind us of our own evil deeds, and of our fathers' deeds which were like ours,*
> *as a consequences of which these tragic afflictions came upon them and upon us. For*
> *as we remember these things we ought to repent and do good.*

Rambam is making clear here that our rituals, observances, prohibitions,
and restrictions are an important means of moving toward *teshuvah*. These actions can *stimulate* the heart and the mind to probe and analyze why these national calamities have befallen us – certainly they are not mere coincidences
or chance encounters with the impersonal forces of history – and therefore,
how we can be transformed by them. After all, if we are merely the victim (or
beneficiary) of chance events, there is nothing to be gained or lost from ex-
amining them. The event and experience cannot – and should not – change
us. It cannot be meaningful at all except in the most immediate and superficial sense.

However, we have stated that mourning is designed to bring about *teshuva*, transformation. By definition then, our loss cannot be chance. It cannot be random. Our loss itself must be meaningful.

The sociological or military or economic factors which play into a particular national event are academic studies best left to the political scientist and sociologist. For the man of faith, these explanations are wholly insufficient. Rambam is clear that to believe that when trouble befalls a community it is merely,

> *the way of the world for such a thing to happen to them, and their trouble is a matter of pure chance, they have chosen a cruel path which will cause them to persevere in their evil deeds.*

*Tzara*, *Churban*, tragedy and oppression do not call for behavior alone. They call for *teshuvah*. They demand the introspection and soul-searching (as individuals and as a people) that can bring about transformation. Just as Rambam states that, "whoever does not mourn in the manner prescribed by the rabbis is cruel" (because it is only through mourning that *teshuvah* can be realized) so too he declares that attributing *Churban* to mere chance is also cruel because one could never attain a real level of understanding in a way that could lead to *teshuvah*.

There is no meaning in random events. There is no significance in chance. The falling of a tree in a forest is meaningless without God, how much more so the falling of a leaf? Without God, murder is meaningless. Death is meaningless. Life, too, must therefore be meaningless.

In such a world, *teshuvah* is not only impossible, it is unnecessary.

Such a worldview is not a Jewish worldview!

God is fully engaged in the Jewish people. He Himself prompts His nation to remember that when "It shall come to pass, when all these things come upon you, the blessings and the curse, which I have set before you… and you shall return unto the Lord you God, and you shall obey His voice."

*I have set before you.*

Could there be a more direct affirmation of God's presence. There are no 'arbitrary' events. No mere 'chance.' God is present. Meaning and faith are possible. As the prophet Jeremiah calls out, "Of what shall a living man complain? A strong man for his sins! Let us search and examine our ways and return to *Hashem*, let us lift our hearts with our hands to God in Heaven: We have transgressed and rebelled; You have not forgiven."

...and return to *Hashem*. *Teshuvah*!

So, if *teshuvah* and transformation are our goals, how do we manage to go forward for our collective community, the people Israel, to go forward in the shadow of *Churban*? Remembrances only heighten our pain and keep us cognizant of our terrible loss. Where is our consolation?

Once again, the answer is to found in the soothing knowledge that man is not alone. God is. God too mourns. He too feels bereft of His glory, and He too recognizes that *Churban* means an obstacle to complete service and a diminution of His splendor on earth.

When He exiled His children from His/their land, He too went into exile – *shechinta begaluta*. The Divine Presence is in exile. *Kol makom sh'galu shechina imaen*. Every place that Jews have been exiled, God is with them.

The *Shechina*, the Divine Presence, is involved with Israel in the misery of their exile.

Israel is never alone. Israel is never without God. When God informs Moshe how He is to be introduced to *B'nai Yisrael* in *Mitzrayim*, He proclaims, "I am that I am." Among the many understandings of this powerful statement of identification is this one in the Talmud, "I will be with them in this sorrow and (*asher*) I will also be with them in the subjugation they will suffer at the hands of other kingdoms."

God readily admits to the necessity of His suffering along with His children. Moreover, God sorrowfully laments every day, three times a day, the destruction and exile He brought upon His children,

> *I hear a divine voice, cooing like a dove, and saying: Woe to the children, on account of whose sins I destroyed My house and burnt My temple and exiled them among the nations of the world!...Not in this moment alone does it so exclaim, but thrice each day does it exclaim thus!*

The Talmud concludes this passage reflecting on God's pain and pangs, with the following insightful and instructive statement about the principle passage of the Kaddish:

> *And more than that, whenever the Israelites go into the synagogues and schoolhouses and respond: "May His great name be blessed!" the Holy One, blessed be He,*

*shakes His head and says: Happy is the King who is thus praised in this House!*
*Woe to the father who had to banish his children, and woe to the children who had*
*to be banished from the table of their father.*

In other words, God *admits* to His own grief and bereavement! He openly
proclaims that He is with His children in their distress, lacking and missing
their company, having been banished from His table. Therefore, ever since
the *Churban* He needs to be ever so much more assured, as it were, that "His
great name be blessed." This passage, more than any other, substantiates the
idea that Kaddish is the vehicle through which the mourning Jew (individually and collectively) hears that message that he is not alone and, not being
alone, can find meaning and, finding meaning, achieves *teshuvah.*

Man is not alone.

Loss and destruction are not suffered by man alone.

Woe not only to the banished children but also to the Father who had to
banish, destroy and exile, and thus cause an insurmountable *Hillul Hashem*
necessitating our renewed and reassuring faith in Him through the recitation
of Kaddish.

According to the R. Hayim of Volozhin, the ultimate reason for man's
prayer is to pray for the removal of the pain and agony caused above when
man suffers below.

*Teshuvah* not only heals us, it heals God as well.

For this reason, God refers to every victory and salvation attained by
Israel when calling upon Him as "My salvation." Is there a clearer statement
that Israel's salvation is His as well? "He will call upon Me and I will answer
him. I am with him in distress, I will release him and I will honor him. With
long life, I will satisfy him, and I will show him My salvation."

God is with us in Israel's distress. Even in the midst of our most devas-
tating exile, a long, dark night with no hope of a coming dawn – just like that
of an individual's travail in the depth of personal grief – the Psalmist offers a
fervent prayer for God's help. "But as for me, I trust in Your kindness: My
heart will exalt in Your salvation…"

Our salvation is God's salvation. Therefore, "I will sing kindly to *Hashem*,
for He has dealt kindly with me."

PRAYER, MOURNING, TESHUVAH –

Prayer's highest level and reason when a man mourns is not to beseech God to simply remove one's personal pain and anguish. Prayer's aim and objective is – particularly when we have desecrated His name, diminished His glory, and caused suffering above, even as we suffer below – for God's own sake. To relieve the suffering above *as we seek* to remove the suffering below. Our suffering is God's merciful way of prodding us to recognize His suffering, so that we would pray.

Prayer, according to R. Hayim of Volozhin, is the mechanism by which man's suffering – a result of his own sins and failings – elevates man to recognize and empathize with the sufferings of the One Above Who shares and pariticipates in man's *tza'ar*. This insight allowed Chazal to declare that whoever involves God in his *tza'ar* will have his *parnasah* doubled, a reward for his own agony, as well as for the agony caused to God.

Is it any wonder then that when man suffers the *Shekhinah* exclaims, "I am burdened by My head, I am burdened by My arm."? Why head and arm? Because they, more than anything else, demonstrate God's complete identification and sympathy with man's suffering. The head and the hand hold man's *tefillin* in place. God, as it were, also dons *tefillin*. Man's hand-*tefillin* symbolizes Israel's love of God, His Unity, and the remembrance of His miracles. The head-*tefillin* symbolizes that Israel adorns itself with God's glory, and His commandments serve as its crown.

God's *tefillin* demonstrate that the One God chose the one Israel, that He raised Israel over all the other nations, that He considers Himself praised when Israel fulfills the commandments. He testifies that His prime desire of creation was that Israel exist and that His original thought in creating the world was to create Israel. In a binding relationship says the Chatam Sofer, each partner wears jewelry as a reminder and declaration of the love each has for the other. This is the symbolism behind both Israel and God wearing *tefillin*.

Our bond is clear. Our relationship is strong.

That bond is damaged when we mourn. When man's world is shattered by the advent of the death of a loved one, he may not don *tefillin*. The relationship between him and God is distanced.

That mutual – and temporary – suspension is man's greatest consolation, both in his personal as well as his national bereavement. Man is not alone. God too cannot don his *tefillin*. God too coos like the dove, saying, "Woe to the father who had to banish his children."

God awaits His nation's proclamation, "May His great name be blessed" as He awaits the individual's same proclamation. *Teshuvah*, transformation, is the essential dynamic of re-establishing the bond with God, more closely than it had existed before..

May His great name be blessed, so that He too may be consoled!

# Prayer and Love

## What It Means to "Love Your Neighbor as Yourself"
## A Meditation

## I.

And the Lord said, Because the cry of Sodom and Gomorrah is great, and because their sin is very grave; I will go down now, and see whether they have done altogether according to the cry, which has come to me; and if not, I will know. And the men turned their faces from there, and went toward Sodom; but Abraham still stood before the Lord. And Abraham drew near, and said, Will you also destroy the righteous with the wicked? Perhaps there are only fifty righteous inside the city; will you also destroy and not spare the place for the fifty righteous who are in it? Be it far from you to do after this manner, to slay the righteous with the wicked; and that the righteous should be as the wicked, be it far from you; Shall not the Judge of all the earth do right? And the Lord said, If I find in Sodom fifty righteous inside the city, then I will spare the whole place for their sakes.. And Abraham answered and said, Behold now, I have taken upon me to speak to the Lord, I who am but dust and ashes; Perhaps there shall lack five of the fifty righteous; will you destroy the whole city for lack of five? And he said, If I find there forty five, I will not destroy it. And he spoke to him yet again, and said, Perhaps there shall be forty found there. And he said, I will not do it for forty's sake. And he said to him, Oh let not the Lord be angry, and I will speak; Perhaps there shall thirty be found there. And he said, I will not do it, if I find thirty there. And he said, Behold now, I have taken upon me to speak to the Lord; Perhaps there shall be twenty found there. And he said, I will not destroy it for twenty's sake. And he said, Oh let not the Lord be angry, and I will speak yet but this once; Possibly ten shall be *found there. And he said, I will not destroy it for ten's sake. And the Lord went his way, as soon as he had left talking with Abraham; and Abraham returned to his place...*

I cannot read this Biblical passage without being astonished by the powerful dynamic that is at play here. Abraham *avinu*, a remarkable man by any estimation, a righteous man, *but a man nonetheless*, engages God – the being who we know to exist *outside* of time and place, that is, outside of man's "playground" – in what, when everything is said and done, amounts to a negotiation.

Astonishing!

While it is perhaps not particularly surprising to read of a situation when man is petitioning God, in this case it is indeed astonishing that, in this passage at least, it appears as if man has the ability to actually influence God!

But how can such a thing be? What might such a thing really mean? For a man to truly influence God's decisions would upend not only the relationship between God and man but would call into deepest question the very nature of each. In such a context, what would it mean to be a man? What would it mean to be God? And yet... read the words of this passage and the simple sense you cannot help but come away with is that Abraham not only negotiates with God but that his argument and pleas hold sway with God and carries the day in God's decision-making.

Such a reading is necessary in the simple sense. But as Ben Bag-Bag exclaims, "Turn it and turn it, for all is in it." The simple reading is never the last word when reading a Biblical passage.

Many readers, when they read this passage, do not focus on Abraham but rather, when they focus on this passage, focus on the "sinfulness" of Sodom and Gomorrah and the ultimate punishment that they will receive as a consequence of that sinfulness. They tend to gloss over the exchange between Abraham and God as if it were ancillary to the primary narrative.

And why not? After all, this is not the first time that the Torah records that God's communication with the first Jew in the Patriarchal narratives is "conversational" in nature. God and Abraham regularly "spoke." Is this passage so terribly different?

Yes. Certainly in terms of what we can learn from it and how it might ultimately inform our meditation on loving one's neighbor. The careful reader would do well to focus his attention closely on the dynamic between God and Abraham here. This "negotiation" over the outcome of the cities of Sodom and Gomorrah is not a conversation as such. It is not a political plea or a legal transaction. It is, quite simply, *prayer* in its most elemental and defining sense – communicating *with* God.

Prayer is many things to many people. But at its heart, regardless of its purpose – to plead, to thank, to honor – it must be a communication with God. A conversation. If it is not this, it is diminished. Yet for the "rational believer" – if such a creature could truly exist – prayer is probably not a conversation *with* God so much as a communication *to* God. They are speaking. They hope that God is listening. But they do not expect God to be truly responsive, to change.

Abraham is a true believer. He does not "hope" that God is listening. He *knows* that God is listening. And so, in this remarkable passage in *Breishit* we see Abraham, the first Jew, not only speaking *to* God but communicating so effectively that God seems to *respond* directly to his appeals.

Doesn't the heartfelt prayer, the prayer uttered with genuine *kavanah*, expect as much? When we cry out to God to show His mercy to a loved one who is ill; when a parent whispers tearful prayers to God to watch over a beloved child; when our daughters' bellies are ready to burst forth with beautiful children and we fear the terrible dangers inherent in that miraculous process of birth... when we speak to God in these and millions of other circumstances, wouldn't we want to be like Abraham and find that God has not only *heard* our pleas but has *listened* to them and has adjusted the world accordingly?

Wouldn't we just?

But *can* we truly influence God in the deepest sense of what it means to influence? Can we *change* God's will ? Of course not. So if Abraham cannot truly change God's decision to destroy Sodom and Gomorrah, what is the true dynamic at play in this passage?

Or, more specifically, What is prayer?

Ah, to quote Hamlet, there's the rub. In reading the story of Sodom and Gomorrah, rather than coming away from Abraham's negotiation with God with the sense that God had changed, is it possible to come away from it with the notion that it was Abraham who had changed?

I believe that must be the case.

There is a lovely passage in "The Little Prince" by Antoine de Saint-Exupéry in which the Little Prince "commands" the sun to rise and to set. Of course, he only does so at the sun's appointed times.

The dock worker stands upon the dock and tosses a line to a boat. The boatman grasps the rope and then the dock worker begins to pull mightily on the boat. Slowly, the boat comes closer to the dock, closer until the boat can be tied off against the dock.

In that dynamic, was the boat drawn to the dock or was the dock drawn to the boat?

The answer is self-evident. As the rope connecting the boat and dock is shortened, the boat is drawn to the dock. Not the other way around. The Little Prince, in "commanding" the sun to rise and set at its appointed hour does not order the sun to keep its daily rhythms. By his commands, he is bringing himself into concert with the sun's rhythms.

So too in prayer.

Abraham's petition to God did not change God's will. It allowed Abraham to come to terms and bring himself into concert with God's will.

Genuine prayer allows us to bring ourselves into concert with God. In doing so, it accomplishes the most important task that exists between God and man – to bridge the distance between us, to draw us closer.

Jewish tradition teaches that prayer is both action and posture, both verb and noun. It bridges and it is the bridge. Prayer is an affirmation of love and faith. When the Torah teaches us *ulevodo bkhol levavkehm*, "loving the Lord your God and serving Him with all your heart and soul," the Talmud asks, "What is service of the heart? What is *avodah shebalev*?"

The Talmud's direct answer is: prayer. As Rambam elaborates in his *Halachic* Code,

> *To pray daily is an affirmative duty, as it is said, "And you shall serve the Lord your God." The service here referred to, according to the teaching of tradition, is prayer. As it is said, "And to serve Him with all your heart," on which the Sages commented, "what may be described as service of the heart? Prayer." The number of prayers is not described in the Torah. No form is prescribed in the Torah. Nor does the Torah prescribe a fixed time for prayer.*

In other words, the very idea of prayer is revealed in the Torah. More importantly, in identifying prayer as the true service of the heart, the Torah reveals the basic human need and instinct to pray. For seeking that "true service" is indeed elemental to who we are as human beings. However, as specific as the Torah is regarding the service of the heart is as vague as it is about its practice. The Torah does not speak of when, where, what, or how one is to pray.

While the Rabbis determined the structure of prayer, one might ask why the Torah remained silent on this important issue. The reason is because prayer, *tefilah*, is never-ending. Our reasons for prayer never cease, therefore neither should our prayer.

We should never cease to be aware that our existence is dependent upon His great mercy. We should never cease to recognize how the distance between us must be bridged. Perhaps this is why our Sages deemed, "were it that man should pray all day long."

Did they mean that man should *literally* engage in the act of prayer all day long? No. Jewish law and tradition make clear that to live full and meaningful lives requires many behaviors that are not prayer, as such. What the Sages *are* saying is that we must always move forward through the world *in a prayerful attitude*, recognizing the need to pray, to ask, to acknowledge and to thank God in every waking moment. And even then, our prayerfulness would not be sufficient, because the purpose of our prayer, of our prayerful stance is to reduce the distance between us and God. Because we can never erase that distance completely, we can never cease to engage in the work to reduce it. That is, we can never cease to pray.

Even if we were to pray all day long, our task would never be complete because the very instant that we "finish" and stop praying, the need begins anew in all its absolute completeness. We never pick up where we left off but always from the beginning.

This is the meaning of the moving and powerful *Birkat Hashir* of *Nishmat*, which we recite specifically at the end of *P'sukei D'zimra* on Shabbat and Yom Tov, when we can reflect more deeply and profoundly about the fundamental dynamic of our faith, that in expressing profound praise and gratitude to God for all that He has done, we must simultaneously affirm our continued dependence upon His mercy. We readily admit that:

*Even if our mouths were full of song as the sea, our tongues full of joyous song as the multitude of waves...we still could never thank God for even one of the thousand, thousand of thousands and myriad, myriads of favors that he performed for us.*

Could there be a more powerful statement that *tefilah* is – and should be – never-ending? All one can do is to pause, to catch one's breath long enough to realize just how much more gratitude, praise, and requests are still due!

This is precisely Rambam's view. *Tefilah* is Biblically ordained (*mitzvah min ha-Torah*) and *tefilah* has no set time. Prayer, the "service of the heart" can never cease, nor can it be contained in a rigid structure – a preordained time or pattern. At its purest, such service should be spontaneous and genuine. To try and contain such heartfelt outpourings in imposed structures would cause the structures to give way and to fail. It would be as if one tried to put sunlight into a box.

Every aspect of our lives should not only *be* prayer in the deepest sense but our prayer should define our conscious response to each and every event and experience of our lives. The *Mishnah* in *Berachot* teaches:

*If a person sees shootings stars, earthquakes, thunder, storms, and lightning, he should say, "Blessed is He whose strength and might fill the world."*

*If he sees mountains, hills, seas, rivers, and deserts, he should say, "Blessed is He who brought about creation."*

*For rain and good tidings, a person should say, "Blessed is He who is good and does good." For evil tidings, he should say, "Blessed be the true Judge."*

Prayer is not only essential for human experience. It is fundamental to all of creation – and to God Himself. The Talmud goes so far as to say that "Even the Holy One, Blessed be He, prays." And what does He pray? "May it be My will that My mercy overcomes My anger, and that My mercy dominates all My attributes so that I may deal with My children mercifully, and for their sake not extract strict justice."

According to the Talmud, the bridge that connects us to God is not a one-way bridge at all.

Prayer then is the constant dynamic of our lives. There is *always* a distance between us and God that we are *always* trying to minimize and bridge. Our only vehicle for doing so is prayer. Yet, how can we constantly pray? We can't if we do not understand that words are *not* the only vehicle for prayer. But to do that, we must first understand why they are.

We have said that prayer is a conversation. But conversations are often informed by much more than words.

When prayers were formalized – their words, the times of their being uttered, the place – they nevertheless required *more than words* in order to be prayer, to be *tefilah*. They required the personal and emotional. They required the spiritual. They required the self-awareness. They required the *self* to be engaged, for the heart to be caught up in the spirit of prayer.

They required *kavanah*. Only through *kavanah*, inspiration, can we know that our hearts and souls are engaged in our prayer. *Rachmanah liba bahe* – God desires and seeks the service of the heart more than the service of the lips. God responds to the cries of our hearts.

Words can be the vehicle for our prayer.

Or, words can be just words.

Recall the lovely story of the grandfather walking in his garden. He was bending to smell the beautiful perfume of his roses when he thought he heard something. He raised himself up and looked around. Yes, he heard something, but what was it? Walking amongst his plants and flowers, he sought out the sound.

He began to smile as he came closer, recognizing the sound of his dear granddaughter sitting in a corner of his garden, singing a song. And not just any song. She was chanting what sounded like a prayer she might have heard in the synagogue. But though the melody was familiar, she was chanting the letters of the alphabet.

"What are we doing?" he asked her, a kindly smile breaking across his face.

She looked up at him and returned his smile. "I am praying," she said earnestly.

His eyes widened. "Yes?"

She nodded. "But I cannot think of exactly the right words so I am just saying all the letters," she explained. "But God, Who knows what is in my heart, will put the words together for me."

The Torah, in revealing the depth of Yitzchak's prayer, teaches: *vayetze Yitzchak lasuach basadeh lifnot erev* – And Isaac went out to stroll (or meditate) in the field at evening time." The Sages understood this to say that Yitzchak actually went out to pray *Mincha*, the afternoon service. They explain that *lasuach*, whose *shoresh* means "to converse" means "prayer" in the Rabbinic tradition.

As the Psalmist writes, "*Tefilah leani ki yaatof velifeni haShem yispoch sicho.*" A prayer of the afflicted when he fails, and pours out his complaint before God. Here, the Psalmist is using the traditional Hebrew poetic technique of parallelism to draw a connection between *tefillah* and *sicho*, prayer and conversation, and making it clear that they are synonyms. (It is not uninteresting that, when Isaac walked in the field, Rebecca first glimpsed him.)

It is still curious, however, why the Torah uses such an unusual term to describe the fact that Yitzchak instituted *Tefilat Mincha*. Why doesn't the Torah simply use the more direct and straightforward, *ledaber* – to speak or to verbalize? Why the term, *lasuakh*, with the meaning "to converse?"

It is because a conversation engages one's total personality. Talking to or being talked to objectifies one or the other, or perhaps both. But a conversation maintains the dignity and mutual respect of all involved in the conversation. Prayer as conversation is a total engagement with God. The truly pious and devout person responds to all of life's situations in a prayerful manner – not merely in a rote, formulaic manner but in an engaged, conversational manner. He does not pray only in the synagogue at set times but his "prayer" is a continual and on-going conversation with God, one that is not restricted by formulaic structures or set times or even words. Like Yitzchak, the devout Jew prays anytime and anyplace – in the field at *mincha* time, before the fall of evening, when prayer is least expected.

A great Chasidic master taught that the deepest meaning of Chazal's statement that *ein sicha ela Tefilah* is that, for Yitzchak, every conversation was a prayer – and every prayer a conversation. Each and every form of communication was a religious and meaningful experience – even when least expected. Such an understanding brings prayer into the world of commerce, into the home, into school, into… into the very fields! The formerly compartmentalized world is made whole and seamless not by its inherent nature but by the strength and power of prayer.

Yitzchak instituted the *Mincha* service to demonstrate clearly that we should *always* engage in prayer, even at times when it might not seem the most natural thing to do. After all, it makes sense that we pray in the morning, when God has just returned our *neshama*, our life and our creativity. It is natural that we would pray at night, when the fearfulness and uncertainty of the dark descends upon us. But in the midst of a busy, active day? In the fields?

Such prayer cannot be entered into formally. Or, in a very strict sense, *entered into*. Such prayer should be a piece of a larger whole; a continuation of an on-going conversation.

The *Baal Torah Temimah* explained that *Mincha* is prayed as the sun begins to set. *Mincha* refers to the fact that *hashemesh nakha*, or said differently, *munach al shiflut veyeridah*, the sun is on the downside, descending, disappearing, leaving us with little light until the moon and stars appear later in the night sky. On the other hand, *Shacharit* is offered when a clear and bright sun has arisen, and *Maariv* is davened when stars have clearly appeared. *Mincha* comes at a time of ambiguity. Is it day or is it night? This, fundamentally, is not simply a question of time but of faith as well. Yitzchak responds for he, uniquely, knows best about ambiguity and uncertainty. He is the survivor of the *Akedah*, more than a witness but less than a full participant in Abraham's test of faith. From Yitzchak we learn the fullness of prayer – spontaneous, unstructured, from the heart.

A more recent form of this powerful and profound *Mincha* was prayed in the midst of the Holocaust by the famous Yossel Rakover in 1943. Like Yitzchak, Rakover also conversed in a field during the *Akedah* of European Jewry.

> *God. You have done everything to make me stop believing in You. Now, lest it seem to You that You will succeed by these tribulations in driving me from the right path, I notify You, God, and God of my Fathers, that it will not avail You in the least. You may insult me. You may castigate me. You may take from me all that I cherish*

*and hold dear in the world... But I will always love You... Eternally praised be the God of truth, of love, who will soon show His face to the world again and shake its foundations with His Almighty voice.*

Rakover identifies the spirit that animates prayer – love. He makes clear that praying to God is the necessary consequence of loving God. Just as prayer is a consequence of our love of God, love is a consequence of our prayer; a necessary result of our complete and genuine faith in God. It is for this reason that prayer (*Shemoneh Esreh*) follows the loving affirmation of our faith (*Shema Yisrael*).

Loving affirmation and then prayer.

Love. Prayer.

It is this progressive relationship which prompted the custom of pious Jews to reaffirm the *mitzvah* of "Love Your Neighbor as You Love Yourself" prior to their prayer service. From this pious perspective, the obligation to love all Jews is the gate that must be unlocked and opened before one may enter in prayer before God, and if such prayer is a continual conversation, then such love must also be a continual and on-going *mitzvah*, so that in one's life the antecedent and consequence cannot be distinguished. Love of neighbor. Prayer. Prayer. Love of neighbor. Rather than a progression, loving your neighbor and praying becomes a continuum. Circular rather than linear. Reaffirming. Aspects of the same thing. Both bridges to God.

Reb Menachem Mendel of Vurka suggests that it is imperative to reaffirm the obligation of *vahavta lereacha kamoha* before beginning one's prayers and to have in mind the welfare and well-being of the *klal*, the collective community. Otherwise, one is left to offer prayer for himself and his selfish needs. One who does so must be considered as *gezel*, theft.

A disciple once asked his rabbi, "In the Talmud we read that Abraham kept all the laws. How can this be, since the Law had not yet been given?" The rabbi looked directly at his disciple. "All that is needed to fulfill the Law is to love God. If you are about to do something and you think it might lessen your love, then you will know it is sin. If you are about to do something and think it will increase your love, you know that your will is in keeping with the will of God. This is what Abraham did."

Nothing exemplifies the love of God as clearly as this anecdote: A learned but selfish man once approached Rabbi Abraham of Stretyn and said, "They say that you give people mysterious drugs and that your drugs are effective. Give me one that I may attain the fear of God."

Rabbi Abraham shook his head. "I don't know any drug for the fear of God," he said. "But if you'd like, I can give you one for the *love* of God."

"That's even better!" cried the man. "Give it to me."

"It is the love of one's fellow man."

## II.

The admonition "not to hate your brother in your heart" is the beginning of a series of moral-ethical injunctions which reach a climax with the imperative to "love your neighbor as you love yourself." The progression is clear. You begin with the double-negative, do **not hate** where not hating defines a first step away from hatefulness, or a negative posture. Moving away from a negative must, by definition, be considered movement in a positive direction. So that, while we may not be impressed by someone whose fundamental stance in life is to "not hate" his neighbor we must still acknowledge that such a stance is a first, important step toward an ethical position in the world.

It is not, after all, an **un**ethical position.

The first step is the negation of a negative. The destination is the embrace of the fullness of a positive; to love one's neighbor as oneself. It makes sense then to assume that the laws *hocheach tochiach et amitecha* – to admonish your neighbor – and *lo tisa alav chet* – not to bear sin because of him – and *lo tikom velo titor et bnai amecha* – not to take revenge nor bear a grudge – must also be related to that initial statement not to hate and the ultimate *mitzvah* to love.

More than a simple progression, the Torah is carving out for us a methodology and approach that allows us to deal with legitimate and recurring natural human events and feelings.

Man hurts, insults and embarrasses his fellow with alarming regularity, giving his fellow ample reason to hate him. The "good" man, however, does not react to the hurt and insult with acts of vengeance. Instead, he swallows his pain and suffers in silence, never allowing his hurt to come to the surface. How commendable, no?

See the "good" man, victimized and yet he does not respond with the meanness and violence that defines his attacker. But our "good" man is only good on the surface. His hurt and anger eat at his soul. His pain might not find external expression but it is powerfully destructive internally. It is for this reason that the Torah instructs that we are not to "hate your brother in your heart."

Hate of any kind and any reason is never sanctioned by the Torah. If and when there is background, situations or reasons that provoke what could result in hatred, the proper Torah response is *hocheach tochiach et amitecha* – admonish your neighbor.

The Torah does not instruct us in ways that are beyond our capability. By defining this "middle ground," the Torah is acknowledging the pain and hurt that many of us feel in our dealings with those around us. Perhaps the saint could genuinely respond to this behavior with love but most of us are not saints. Still, we are forbidden to react with violence.

What can a reasonable and good person do? We can certainly acknowledge the hurtfulness of the situation and the *wrongness* of the feelings that our neighbor's behavior caused. We can *admonish*. We can take our neighbor to task *for his behavior*. To admonish is not merely a salve for our feelings, a "band aide" to place over our hurt feelings. Not, to swallow those feelings only hurts us more deeply. We must have an outlet for our legitimate hurt and anger, and *appropriate* outlet. The Torah provides for such an outlet, at the same time providing for constructive criticism of the one who has hurt us so that he can be lovingly taught why and how he erred and sinned.

The fact is, says the Avnei Ezel, that only the person who cares for a fellow Jew, who is concerned for his fellow Jew's way of life, who suffers when another Jew fails – only such a Jew will care enough to share constructive criticism with his fellow Jew, and that kind of *tochacha* will be most effective because it comes from love. Therefore, the Torah teaches, *lo tisna et achikha*. After all, he is your brother, and you must love your brother. So when your brother fails, when he is down, *hocheach tochiach* – admonish him. Not to do so taints you with his sin. *Velo tisa alav chet* – and do not bear sin because of him.

Open, honest, concerned and loving communication – *hocheach* – among humans allows for communication that is not merely reassuring but also instructive, it creates communication that is not just "ideal" but also practical. The ability to criticize out of love rather than out of anger and hatred averts the future guilt of "carrying sin." Indeed, the verb *hocheach* carries not just the sense of criticism or admonition but also of open, honest communication. Abraham addressed Avimelech openly and honestly, not only because he was concerned for himself and his loved ones but also because he understood that such an approach could prevent Avimelech from carrying out his devious intentions, and avoid the hatred that Abraham would then have to bear in his own heart – *vehochiach Avraham et Avimelech.*

What is it that leads a Jew to stand opposed to the natural tendency to respond in kind when he is insulted and hurt? Why should the Jew turn away from the natural, human tendency to hate, to bear a grudge, to take revenge? Because the ultimate goal and benefit of standing opposed to this natural response would be, an opposition that finds its most basic voice in "not hating" is not simply as series of double negatives – *not* to take revenge, *not* to hate, *not* to bear the sin – nor is it the mere "positive" need to admonish or offer constructive criticism. The goal is a more lofty and exalted one. To love.

Love your neighbor as you love yourself.

As much as we are driven by our animal, base instincts we are also called by the grace of our Creator. Yes, we have to overcome our instinct to hate, to respond in kind. But we are also reflections of a brighter light.

What self-respecting person would be satisfied to conduct his life merely as a series of double-negatives? Who seeks a life of mere avoidance of the negative? What kind of life would that be?

Every normal human being seeks – indeed, *needs* – positive reinforcement. He needs acceptance, tolerance, forgiveness, patience, love. None of these can be defined as the negative of its opposite. To suggest that acceptance is the same as "not being shunned," or that forgiveness is the same as "not being blamed" is farcical. These positive, human needs rise to a qualitative level that far exceeds any double-negative.

Recognizing this, the Torah first articulates a process that begins with the avoidance of the negative but which, in its most brilliant and ultimate emanation, is revealed as the most positive statement of human posture in the world possible.

To love.

We all need to know we are loved as surely as we need air to breathe and water to drink. It is a vital, fundamental, *physical, spiritual and emotional* need.

It is true that we sometimes require admonition. We benefit from constructive criticism. We are reassured in knowing that we are not hated. But it is only *by being loved* that we realize the fullness of what it means to be human.

The ultimate *mitzvah* then is to "love your neighbor…" It is nothing less than the cornerstone of Torah and the Jewish faith. Rabbi Akiva taught that it is, "the great general principle of the Torah."

A famous Talmudic episode tells of a prospective convert coming to both Shammai and Hillel, willing to convert if he could be taught the "whole of Judaism" while standing on one foot.

Shammai sent him away but Hillel said, "What is hateful to you, do not do to your neighbor. The rest is commentary. Now, go and master it." The *Targum Yonatan* uses this expression in translation of the verse, "love your neighbor as yourself." So, it is clear from this that Hillel, and the continuum of Jewish tradition, sees the entire Torah encapsulated in the command to, "love your neighbor."

Hillel's response however, suggests that the Torah commandment is fraught with emotional and practical difficulties. After all, he restates the Torah command *but in the negative.* He knows that it is man's tendency to care more about himself than others –*adam karov le'atzmo.* That is the rabbinic, *halachic* position. "Your life takes precedence over your fellow man's." It must be thus. We are unable to truly love if we do not love ourselves first. We cannot value others if we do not value ourselves. And yet… and yet despite this necessity of predominance, the Torah obligates us to love our fellow man *as ourselves.* This seems to go against nature. How could we, beings who are by instinct, designed to place ourselves first, place someone else not above us but equal in our love to ourselves?

It seems impossible. But it cannot be impossible. That is our quandary. For the Torah would not instruct us to do something beyond our capabilities. It must be doable to love our neighbor as ourselves. The difficulty then must be in understanding exactly what is meant by this command.

In an effort to reconcile what seemed to be impossible, many commentaries sought to limit the application of the text, either by limiting what was meant by "neighbor" or, of greater concern, limiting what was meant by "love."

Ramban noted that it is psychologically impossible to feel about one's neighbor as one feels for one's self.

*The phrase, "love thy neighbor as thyself" is not meant literally, since man cannot be expected to love his neighbor as his own soul. Rabbi Akiva himself ruled the contrary, that "your life takes precedence over your fellowman's.*

Ramban therefore suggests on the basis of the letter *lamed* in the word *lereacha* that the phrase actually means love *for* your neighbor, and therefore the Torah is teaching that "we should wish our neighbor to enjoy the same that we wish for ourselves."

Such an understanding suggests that we should want for our neighbor as much as we want for ourselves, without restriction, jealousy, or selfishness.

*But a man should wish his fellow well in all things, just as he wishes his own self and have no reservations.*

Ramban's perspective seems to validate Hillel's rendering of the whole of the Torah while on one foot – an admonition couched in the negative, "what is hateful to you, do not do to your fellow." Ibn Ezra likewise explains that the Torah intends one to like what is good for one's friend the way one likes it for one's self. That was likely Onkelos' view when he translated, "love your neighbor as yourself…" as "and you shall have mercy on your friends as you have mercy on yourself."

Ramban codified the *mitzvah* of loving your neighbor in precise *halachic* terms, setting boundaries which are both "realistic" and "achievable":

*It is incumbent on everyone to love every Israelite as one's self, since it is said, "You shall love your neighbor as yourself." Thus, one ought to speak in praise of one's neighbor and be careful of one's neighbor's property as one is careful of one's property, and solicitous about one's honor.*

Animating all these perspectives on this *mitzvah* is the difficulty the commentators have with the concept of "love" and its possibility in the purest sense. From their perspective, to love another in the same manner as one loves himself is beyond realistic expectations. It was in response to this understanding that Ramban capped the views of these *Rishonim* by at the least setting some concrete guidelines, guidelines which seem to be consistent with Hillel's principle of not doing to another what is hateful to you.

There is much to praise in this worldview. If one lives by Ramban's parameters then one would live an ethical life – he would not steal, damage, insult, or demean a fellow human being. In other words, he would not do those things which he would not want done to him.

The question is, whether the sum total of what one does *not* do adds up to what one actually *does*.

The Torah command is to *do* the *positive*, not to *not* do the *negative*. "Love your neighbor as yourself" is not the same thing as "what is hateful to you, do not do to your fellow."

The Torah commands that we *love*. The practical application of the *mitzvah* (*ma'aseh hamitzvah*) may very well be achieved through not harming, injuring, etc. However, not doing the negative is supposed to be the consequence of fulfilling the *mitzvah*, not the result of it.

As to the question whether it is within the realm of human possibility to love one's *re'ah* as much as one's self, an approach is offered by the *Ba'al ha-Turim* and Ibn Ezra that does point to a human situation which allows for a complete and literal fulfillment of the *mitzvah*. Both commentaries interpret *re'ah* as referring to one's wife, whom it is possible, nay, presumed one would love *kamocha*. *Halachic* substantiation of this view is found in several Talmudic passages:

> *A man is forbidden to perform his marital duty in the daytime, for it is said, "You shall love your neighbor as yourself." But what is the proof? Abaye replied: "He might observe something repulsive in her and she would thereby become loathsome to him."*

The requirement to see a woman prior to marrying her is likewise connected to this source.

> *A man may not betroth a woman before he sees her, lest he subsequently see something repulsive in her, and she then becomes loathsome to him, and the all Merciful has said, "You shall love your neighbor as yourself."*

The point here is that it is inherent in marriage, whose love knows no bounds, is the possibility to positively fulfill the Torah's command, "to love

your *re'ah* as yourself." In regard to one's wife not only is the reason and mo-
tivation one of love, so is the actual application and fulfillment of the *mitzvah*.
Therefore, *Baal haTurim* derives from the verse that one who loves his wife
should not engage in conjugal relations with her while having his eye on
someone else, and should not force his wife to have conjugal relations with
him. Doing so would be contrary to the basic sense of love *kamokha*.

## III.

While the love of marriage certainly fulfills the definition of love, it seems
that limiting the Torah command to that singular relationship misses the
Torah's intent. Indeed, rabbinic tradition enlarges the scope of the command
far beyond the marriage bonds. The Talmud deems that when one was deserving of the death penalty, the place of stoning was to be twice the person's
normal height. Similarly, when the death penalty was to be exacted by sword,
it was to be administered from the neck so that the death should occur more
speedily, "a more easy death." This same dynamic animates the practice of
drugging the guilty person prior to the administration of the death penalty,
so that the pain involved be eased or dulled. Each of these *halachic* stipula-
tions was derived from the command "to love one's neighbor as yourself."

Certainly these examples, in which the loving of a fellow applies even to
those guilty of the most heinous crimes makes clear that the command to love
one's neighbor applies in circumstances far beyond the unique bonds of marriage. Which brings us back to Hillel's "Torah on one foot." "To love…" is a
positive injunction. Hillel's formulation "not to do what is hateful" is not. It
is couched in the double-negative. As such, it does not rise to the level of the
Torah's injunction.

Reb Yisrael Salanter (in the *Sefer Beit Yitzchak*) relates the story of a preacher
who sought to deliver a *drasha* in the *beit midrash* of the learned philanthropist
Reb Tzvi Novioski. Reb Tzvi, who spent his time learning Torah, refused to
have the *darshan* preach, as this would interrupt his learning. The preacher
protested, claiming that he must preach so that he may then earn the monies
collected on his behalf at the conclusion of the *drasha*.

Overhearing this discussion, Reb Salanter addressed Reb Tzvi and said
that Hillel could not state his principle in the positive mode, that is, "not doing

what is hateful" could not be rendered "what is good for you, do unto your neighbor" because not all that is good for one is necessarily good for another. Reb Israel cited Reb Tzvi's argument with the preacher as a perfect case in point. "there is no doubt that you prefer to learn and that is good for you. However, to tell the needy preacher not to preach so that you might continue your learning is certainly not in the realm of good."

"What you must consider," he continued, "is whether you would be pleased if harm would result from that which is good for yourself. "This," he emphasized, "is the ultimate gauge which must be used to measure and verify all interpersonal deeds and relationships, to determine whether or not they are truly good. That is what Hillel meant when he said not to wrong or harm a neighbor, even if you will benefit thereby."

Reb Salantar's point was that no individual has the right – or, more correctly, the perspective – to measure any good or benefit through the lens of his own narrow needs and benefits. Any one individual's worth, existence, or needs can only be valued in relations to the *klal*. The individual as a *prat* has no meaning or worth. Reb Yerucham Leibovitz explained (in *Sefer Da'at Torah*), that this truth can be compared to a large tree with many branches and leaves. The survival of any one branch or leaf is completely dependent on the larger tree itself. So too, the individual's survival, his benefit, can only be dependent on the survival and benefit of the larger *klal*. No one should exclude himself from the group of *mevarchim*. Even the impression (fair or not) of exclusion from the *klal* cannot be tolerated or condoned.

In this context, we can see that Hillel's precept cannot be simply translated into a positive but rather that his teaching is that the command to "love your neighbor" cannot be realized through the mere avoidance of jealousies, nor does it mean that we may not insult or cause hurt to any man. He is teaching that we must always see ourselves as part of the whole and that *kamocha* should always serve as our guiding principle in guiding our behavior and relationships. *Kamocha* does not measure or reveal how far and to what extent one is to love, rather it informs us that our fellow is *kamocha*, he is a human being "just like you," part of the *klal* and, as such, deserving no less care and consideration.

This understanding of *kamocha* seeks to accomplish in relationships between human beings the same thing that prayer does between God and man

– bridging the distance that, left to base and basic tendencies, would never be bridged.

The *Biur* focuses on this *kamocha* element:

*The word* kamocha *is not usually used adverbially but rather adjectivally, meaning "similar to you." Love thy neighbor who is as thyself. Every man was created in the image of God. Love him therefore offers us no advice on how far to go, in loving our neighbor. It merely tells us to love our neighbor who is a human being, "just like you." The Hebrew phrase for loving a person as one's self, is indeed employed elsewhere, in the case of David and Jonathan, where it states that the latter loved David "as his own soul"* (ke-nafsho).

Nechama Leibowitz points out that this approach is also found in the Torah's instruction regarding attitudes to be shown to the stranger in society:

*The stranger who resides with you shall be treated the same as the native born, and you shall love him as yourself; for you were strangers in the land of Egypt.*

The end of the verse, which points out that we too were strangers once, in the land of Egypt, and that that experience should inform our understandings of ourselves and of how we are to treat others, makes sense *only* if we interpret *kamocha* to mean that the stranger is in need of greater help, understanding and sensitivity – just as we did when we found ourselves in a similarly vulnerable position in Egypt.

*Kamocha.* What another feels is a human feeling. We are human. Therefore, inherently and through experience, we understand the feelings of another. Because we understand, that understanding must inform our behavior.

The stranger is *kamocha.* He is like us. We *understand.* How much more should we understand our "neighbor"? How much more should that understanding inform our behavior? Understanding is the heart that beats in the soul of love. Once we understand, we can love. The stranger is *kamocha* just as the neighbor is *kamocha.* This truth calls on us to understand and to love.

It is also a profound statement that none of us is alone. We are always in a *klal.* For everyone around us is *kamocha.*

Rabbi Joseph B. Soloveitchik views the Egyptian exile as the "experience which molded the moral quality of the Jewish people for all time." The *Galut* experience "taught the Jew ethical sensitivity, what it truly means to be a Jew. It sought to transform the Jew into a *rachaman*, one possessing a heightened form of ethical sensitivity and responsiveness." The most immediate and practical way to teach this sensitivity and compassion – an *imo anochi betzara* approach – is by recalling one's own experience of *tzara*, of pain and loneliness, of oppression, of feeling the distance between yourself and your fellow. Recalling that feeling fills one with compassion for others, with the desire to alleviate similar feelings in our fellow.

The more immediate the experience or the greater the understanding, the better one is able to bridge the gap between himself and his fellow. For this reason, one who has suffered illness is often best at understanding the agony of the ill. The one who has suffered the loss of a loved one can best comfort the bereaved.

The *Galut* experience, which we all experience, is the first step in bonding, the first link in the *klal* chain. That experience sharpens and refines the Jewish ethical sensitivity and moral awareness. It does not allow us to close our eyes to the suffering of those *kamocha*, to our fellow human beings.

The *Galut* defines our moral and ethical imperative to our fellow. "You shall not pervert the justice due a stranger or to the fatherless; nor take a widow's garment in pawn."

Why not?

*Because you were strangers in the land of Egypt!* Because you were slaves and it was not through your own strength or intelligence or wealth that you were freed. Rather, it was because, "the Lord your God redeemed you."

Thirty-six times the Torah exhorts us to treat the stranger kindly. Thirty-six times. Why? *Ki gerim heitem be'eretz Mitzrayim* – because you were strangers in the land of Egypt. *Veatem yedatem et nefesh ha-ger* – you *know* the soul of the stranger! Having experienced estrangement and discrimination, having suffered the pangs of loss, you understand. Therefore, you can love.

*Kamocha.*

The Torah teaches us not to work the servant "with rigor;" not to assign the *eved* work that would "break him" – *lo tirde bo befavech*. The term, *befavech*, appears only two other times in the Torah and in both those instances it refers to the back-breaking labors imposed upon the Israelites in Egypt.

Our experience in Egypt is not to teach merely to have the capacity to love. It places in our hearts the *necessity* to love, to sympathize, to share. To build a bridge to another and to reduce the distance between ourselves and our fellows. We are all, after all, branches of one tree.

The prophet Isaiah proclaims, "Behold, I have refined you, but not as silver; I have tried you in the furnace of afflictions." The Torah declares, "But you, the Lord took and brought you out of Egypt, that iron furnace, to be His people of inheritance as you are this day."

And what kind of people did God bring us out of Egypt to be? *Kedoshim!*

The imperative to "love your neighbor" along with the series of other ethical-moral injunctions make up the opening of the *sidra Kedoshim*. These *mitzvot* were spoken by Moses "unto all the congregation of the children of Israel." Rashi took note of this all-embracing expression and comments:

*that this chapter was delivered in full assembly since most of the fundamental rulings of the Torah are derived therefrom. Moshe, speaking "unto all the congregation of the children of Israel" meant that he taught these laws to the entire assembled collective community of Israel, together and not in separate groups as he normally taught them.*

This series of ethical injunctions includes appeals to demonstrate kindness to the weak, respect to the aged, and to refrain from bearing a grudge, injunctions which culminate in the crowning statement, "to love your neighbor as yourself."

There can be no question that this injunction refers not only to the marriage relationship, or even to the Jewish community but rather to the *klal gadol*, to the community of fellow people. Still, there remains the question, Why would Moses change his manner of teaching this set of *mitzvot* from every other? His normal method was to teach each group of the Children of Israel according to their capacity and intelligence. Yet, in the case of *Kedoshim* injunctions, he felt compelled to deviate from his normal practice. This only reinforces the understanding that these powerful injunctions in general and their culminating statement in particular demand a *klal*, a collective approach, not only in their practice but in their presentation as well. The *Chatam Sofer* noted that the ideals of the *Kedoshim* laws can only be achieved through a com-

plete immersion in and identification with the needs and goals of the collective community.

No selfish person could fully grasp, let alone implement, these powerful
statements.

It is only through the power and force of *klal* that the *prat* can become holy.
The *Sfat Emet* adds that the *behakhel* approach to the teaching of *Kedoshim*
makes clear that it is only through the unity of the *klal* that genuine *kedusha*
can be achieved. The noble goals outlined in *Kedoshim* not only *can* be but *must*
be achieved by everyone, not just a select few. For this reason, Moses taught
these laws to everyone at the same time, to the priests, the Levites, the elders
and the community at large. Everyone. There was no discrimination, no dif-
ferentiation. Everyone received and understood the message of the *Kedoshim*
laws equally. And everyone was expected to fulfill them *in their plain, uncom-
plicated meaning*. These laws were direct and clear. Everyone could understand.
Everyone could behave in accordance with the laws.

Not everyone could become the *Gadol ha-dor* but every single member of
the *klal* could attain *kedusha* and impart love to his fellow. Perhaps this understanding animates Ben Azzai's rationale in disagreeing with Rabbi Akiva
regarding "the fundamental principle of the Torah." Whereas Rabbi Akiva
was of the opinion that "love your neighbor as yourself" is the foundational
principle, Ben Azzai maintained that "This is the book of the generations of
man" (*Bereshit* 5:1) is the fundamental principle.

Ben Azzai elaborates this view in the *Midrash*:

*That you should not say, since I am despised let my neighbor be similarly despised,
since I am cursed, let my neighbor be similarly cursed. Said Rabbi Tanhuma: If you
act thus, know whom are you despising,* "in the likeness of God made He
him."

Here, Ben Azzai is consistent with Moses when he taught "all the congregation of the children of Israel." He makes no distinctions, differences, or ex-
ceptions made in regard to loving. Elders, priests, and the common man – all
*kamocha*. Even one who denies himself that respect and dignity is not to deny
it to his neighbor. Because of this, Ben Azzai claimed that the text attested to
the common origin of man, created in the image of God, to be the great unifying principle of Judaism. Such a principle requires no interpretation, expla-

nation or exegesis of the kind Hillel's does. This principle is a direct statement. For Ben Azzai, the truth is equally direct. Why are we all expected to be *kedoshim* and therefore, love *kamocha*? Because "I, the Lord your God, am holy" and because we are all, every one of us, created in that holy image.

The powerful statement, "to love your neighbor as yourself" concludes with that most powerful of statements: *Ani Hashem*. I am *Hashem*.

Our love of our fellow man is firmly rooted in our love of God.

## IV.

In his *Miktav M'eliyahu*, Rabbi Eliyahu Dessler speaks of three ascending levels in the observance of "loving your neighbor" in which one's ascension corresponds to the greater identification and *mitgefil* with each individual member of *Klal Yisrael*:

The first, and most basic, level was articulated by Ramban, "*The phrase "love your neighbor as yourself" is not meant literally, since man cannot be expected to love his neighbor as his own soul.*" The Torah recognizes that, *sometimes a person will be interested in his neighbor's welfare in certain respects only; he may wish him wealth, but not scholarly attainment and the like. But even if he wishes him well in everything, in wealth, honor, learning, and wisdom, he will still not want him to be absolutely equal with him.*

It is human nature for every man to seek superiority over his fellow in some aspect of experience. We instinctively struggle for the corresponding recognition, believing this will establish our own uniqueness and identity within society. Without such efforts, we fear we do not possess a singularity which distinguishes us from others. We fear being lost in the multitude of our fellows. Of course, in truth our singularity resides in the quality that we share with all our fellows, that we are created in the image of God. It is this which informs the command to "love your neighbor." Ramban explained that our fears are the result of our baser, more animalistic instincts.

A man should wish his fellow well in all things, just as he wishes his own self and have no reservations. Torah wants for man to know that one's own sense of worth and honor is never negated or diminished by the accomplishments of others.

The second level of "loving your neighbor" relies on the identification of "your neighbor" with "yourself" in an almost literal manner. "By giving to him of yourself you will find in your soul that you and he are indeed one; you will feel in the clearest possible manner that he really is to you "as yourself." In this regard, such love is a pure bridge, bridging the divide between you and your fellow. The world depends on the ability to give. Without this generous, human quality no one would marry or have children. Yet for most people, the ability to love and give is, at best, limited to a small circle of relatives and friends. All others are viewed as strangers and relationships with them are based on taking, on exploitation, and on greed.

> *If one were only to reflect that a person comes to love the one to whom he gives, he would realize that the only reason the other person seems a stranger to him is because he has not yet given to him; he has not taken the trouble to show him friendly concern. If I give to someone, I feel close to him; I have a share in his being. It follows that if I were to start bestowing good upon everyone I come into contact with, I would soon feel that they are all my relatives, all my loved ones. I now have a share in them all; my being has extended into all of them.*

Therefore, Rabbi Dessler concludes, one who has been granted the merit to reach this sublime level can understand the *mitzvah* "love your neighbor" in its literal sense, "without distinction; as yourself: in actual fact."

While it seems instinctual to distinguish between the self and "the other" or the stranger, in commenting on the verse, "You shall not take vengeance, nor bear a grudge," the Jerusalem Talmud makes clear that such distinctions are artificial. If an individual were in the midst of cutting meat and, by accident, cut one hand, would that individual contemplate, as an act of revenge, cutting the hand that cut the first hand? Of course not. They are clearly two parts of the same body. So too is each person part of a larger *klal*. If one deals lovingly and kindly with all Jews, he is one with them, to the point that he couldn't possibly bring himself to avenge or take revenge.

Even so, there is yet another level, a highest level, of *loving one's neighbor*, where the love of one's neighbor emanates *from* one's love and attachment to God.

> *That you should not say, since I am despised let my neighbor be similarly despised, since I am cursed, let my neighbor be similarly cursed. Said Rabbi Tanhuma: If you act thus, know whom are you despising,* "in the likeness of God made He him."

The Rikanti comments that, "one who loves his fellowman created in the image of God loves God and respects Him. This then is the love of one's fellow that is rooted in love of God. One who surrenders himself and his will to God will likewise surrender himself to his fellow man *created in God's image*. The ability to show humility before God and before one's fellow are directly related.

In light of this, Rabbi Akiva views the imperative *"you shall love"* as a basic requisite and need to give love "without distinction." Rabbi Tanhuma adds that *reacha* and *kamocha* must become one and the same, each are reflections of the Divine image.

## V.

The ability to love one's fellow without distinction is compromised by our base, animalistic natures, which demand that we place ourselves at the center of the universe, all-important and all-consuming. Even in *Gan Eden, Chava*, God's own creation and Adam's life partner, gave Adam of the *etz hadaat* "in order that she should not die and he would live, and then marry another woman."

Our desire for distinction, for glory, so often pushes all other things aside. Why then did God create His glory of creation – human beings – with such a powerful and relentless need to establish his self above all other things? Simply because, in the creation, this drive is necessary so that, through its strength and power, people would attain the highest level possible of *avodat ha'shem*.

Six things were said about man. In regard to three, he is like the ministering angels. In regard to three, he is like the beasts. Rabbi Adin Steinsaltz considered this balance and tension in the human psyche:

*This combination of angel and beast is only one of the strange and various combinations forming man. Angel and beast are incompatible contrasts, but in man they are created into a many-faced unity. The combining of the material, bestial body with the angelic, Divine soul, is characteristic of man's combination of contrasts. Flesh and soul, good and evil, are different names for the same things. Within their existence in man, there is no possibility of clearly defining the relations between them, although each of them has for itself a very clear and defined essentiality.*

The Torah itself accounts for this duality in man. "God formed man out of the dust of the ground, and breathed into his nostrils a breath of life." Man is both a natural being and a product of heavenly matter. He resides in the animal kingdom but he is also a transcendental creature, capable of glimpsing the Divine and living accordingly. All of life is a process to reconcile these two natures, and to hew our paths closer to the Divine than to our base natures.

It is our moral sense, our spiritual sense, that allows us to choose; to choose to live as a simple, corporeal being or to climb to transcendental heights. This is the essence of free will.

This dynamic is embodied in the Days of Awe bracketed by Rosh Hashanah and Yom Kippur. Rosh Hashanah focuses on the "*rosh*" – the source of human intellect. The shofar call for *teshuvah* on Rosh Hashanah emanates not from *vidui* or fasting, not from the deprivation of the body and its animalistic needs and physical instincts. Rather, on Rosh Hashanah, we recall the words of the prophet: "Shall the shofar be blown in the city and the nation will not tremble?"

Yom Kippur, on the other hand, incorporates a sense of regret and remorse which emanates from our inability to fully control the base nature inherent in our being. Thus, as the gates of *teshuvah* are about to be closed, we humbly declare:

> *Not in the merit of our righteousness do we cast our supplications before You, but in the merit of Your abundant mercy. What are we? What is our life? What is our kindness? What is our righteousness? What is our might?... For most of their deeds are desolate and the days of their lives are empty before you. The preeminence of man over beast is nonexistent for all is vain.*

Soon after we declare our insignificance, recognizing that our bodies' ultimate end is the maggot and worm, we triumphantly cry out, "You set man apart from the beginning and You considered him worthy to stand before You."

We have wrestled with the angel and beast within our beings. We have acknowledged our baseness and recognized that our worthiness is not our own but rather the result of God setting us apart.

We live in the physical world, with our days and hours taken up in a constant struggle with the base and Divine in our natures. We have two concrete methods to weigh in on the side of the Divine: prayer and *"love your neighbor as yourself."* And of the two, love of our neighbor is the process through which we can arrive at the highest level of *ahavat Hashem* – and bridge the gap not just between ourselves and our fellows, but ourselves and God.

In this way, *"love your neighbor"* becomes prayer.

If we are to attain our goal of *ahavat Hashem* then *"love your neighbor"* would have to remain the achievement of the y*echidei segulah*. Personalities pure and untarnished, as Rav Kook could faithfully declare and call heavens and earth to attest that:

> my love is abundant, literally with all my heart and soul, for our entire nation and all of its denominations. In each faction and in each group there are certainly things with which I cannot agree. This cannot however, cause the flame of love burning within me for our people and all its parts, to be diminished even by a hair's breath. It is sustained within me equally for those who respect me and for those who despise me. I love all of them without limits.

But what are lesser personalities to do when attempting to develop and achieve synonymity between love of God and man? What mechanism is available to aid the "plain Jew" who is seeking to fulfill the commandment to *"love your neighbor"* as a result of his love of God? Is such a goal beyond the reach of the ordinary Jew?

No. And the reason it is not is prayer. It is through prayer, more so than any other religious activity that man is able to achieve companionship with God. Prayer, the Rav explained, "is a dialogue not a monologue. A dialogue exists when one person addresses another, even if the other is temporarily silent."

In prayer, we do not seek a response to a particular request as much as we desire fellowship with God. Could God's response to Job, "where were you when the foundations of the earth were laid?" have satisfied Job's request for witness? Of course not. But God's response affirmed to Job that fellowship with Him existed. And that was enough.

When we pray, God emerges out of transcendence and forms a companionship with us; the infinite and the finite meet and vast chasm is bridged. Or, as we saw in the passage whereby Abraham pleaded the case for the salvation of Sodom and Gomorrah, the process of prayer draws us closer to God as a boat being drawn to the dock.

How do we know how to pray? God Himself taught us how.

*David knew that the Temple was destined to be destroyed and that the sacrificial system would be abolished as s result of the iniquities of Israel. David was distressed for Israel. With what would they effect atonement? The Holy One, blessed be He, said, "When troubles come down upon Israel because of their iniquities, let them stand together before Me as one band and confess their iniquities before Me and recite before Me the order of the* selichot *and I will answer them...Rabbi Johanan said, "The Holy One, blessed be He, revealed this in the verse 'and the Lord passed before him and proclaimed, the Lord, the Lord, manifest and gracious.' This teaches that the Holy One, blessed be He, descended from the mist like a* shaliach tzibur*, enveloped in his* talit*, stood before the ark and revealed to Moses the order of the* selichot.

God, aware of man's frailty and fragility, shows man in a very specific way and with specific words how to approach Him in prayer! Appearing as a *shaliach tzibur* – enveloped in a *talit* – He was instructing His nation to, first and foremost, stand united and together in confession and prayer and He will answer.

Through prayer, man bridges the distance to God. It draws him nearer to the One who first breathed life into Adam. As Rav Kook explained: the individual will is absorbed in its Root. "Man's will is bound to the will of God."

Man's prayer will be effective to the degree that he expresses this identification and concentrates upon understanding that we have no will other than revelation from the light of the Divine Will. Did not Abraham accomplish as much in his petition? The private will is not isolated; it is a branch of the general. In proportion to the degree of closeness between the individual will and the sacred general will, the former is raised and ability of the worshiper to express himself is thereby strengthened – and his prayer is answered.

The prayer experience allows for any abyss between man and God to be bridged. "O, You Who hears prayer, to You does all flesh come."

Rav Kook made clear that man's ability through prayer to achieve an "exalted condition" removes any gulf between God and himself. "The gulf between God and the world is solely a factor of man's knowledge, his perception and the way that he lives."

The abyss is created by man's focus on the "self" and his false perception that his will is separate and apart from His will.

*In man's most exalted condition and in his most perfect insight, he finds that everything is contained in God, that the individuality of everything that exists is nothing but a revelation of divinity, shining forth in different guises.*

What is this exalted condition and the perfect insight that results in "guiltless" prayer? It is the attainment of the highest level of *"love your neighbor… kamocha"*, where love of man emanates from love of God. Then there is no abyss, and God and man are both crowned daily, because man is but a reflection of His Divine image. This bond and companionship can neither tolerate nor allow you to do to your neighbor that which is hateful to you. The infinite and the finite meet, the fast chasm is bridged, the natural response then can only be love, the necessary prelude – and result – of prayer.

# WE ARE
## AS WE ARE NOT

### A MEDITATION ON THE POWER OF PARADOX
### IN JEWISH TRADITION

How do we know who we are? What we are? How do we know who we are *supposed* to be?

How do we *know* anything?

Perhaps the observant Jew could provide an adequate answer. He might tell us that we know who we are and who we are supposed to be because God tells us. God tells us we are to be holy because God is holy.

Those of us who seek to be wise as well as observant, who seek understanding as well as knowledge would find such a response dissatisfying. We know that, like so many matters of real significance, while the easy answer seems so accessible and so right, upon closer scrutiny, it proves to be at once trivially true and maddeningly elusive.

We are dissatisfied because God's message to us is at once straightforward and couched in contrasts; sometimes as simple as a child's arithmetic and other times as infuriatingly complex as a Zen koan . As a consequence, we discover that giving voice to the deepest questions and concerns often finds us speaking in contradictions and in the negative voice. That is, I am this *because* I am _not_ that.

As frustrating as this may be, it is only when we relieve ourselves of simple, declarative statements and lose ourselves in the shadows of contrast that we can begin to find meaning and understanding. As it turns out, the fullness of who I am can only have meaning and find its expression in the context of the emptiness around me.

Self-definition is almost exclusively the function of negation. In other words, I am who I am *only* in the context of what I am not. As Jews, this should be intuitively clear. We Jews, called apart by God to be a holy people, know that we find our most profound sense of self as a people "called apart" – in the distinction between "us" as a holy people… and "them"; those who are not holy.

Yes, our task as a community and as individuals is to be holy. But to fully understand what that means is to engage in a dance with shadows. It is to embrace a world of contrasts.

INTRODUCTION –

If we hope to appreciate the fundamental truths and principles of Judaism, to understand ourselves as Jews in the world that God has created, then we must come to terms with paradox and with the interplay of opposites.

For the believers in the trivially true, the ones who hold that living life can be reduced to a straightforward formula, such paradoxes are distractions. But for those of us who care deeply about what God would have us *be* as well as what God would have us *do* then we must recognize that these paradoxes and conflicts are anything but ancillary to Judaism.

They are fundamental to it.

In order to understand who we are as Jews demands that, like Jacob wrestling with God, we wrestle with the distinctions and contrasts that God has woven into the fabric of life. To do so does not put us outside the stream of traditional Judaism. It places us directly into the swirling, churning currents of who we are.

As we pray our morning prayers, our first *bakasha* – plea – is a request for wisdom and understanding. Dear God, please confer upon us wisdom and understanding. Could we request a more noble gift? Yet, the very words of our prayer hint at what it means to have wisdom and understanding.

In our prayer, we plead for the ability "to *distinguish* day and night." [italics mine] That is, to be wise and understanding is to be able to differentiate between polar opposites.

How many Jews pray this prayer day by day without being astonished by these words and their meaning? How many times have I spoken these very words to God in so perfunctory a manner as to miss their power and significance?

Why have I never protested to God, Where is the wisdom in being able to tell the difference between the day and the night? A young child is able to make such a distinction; *does* make such a distinction all the time. So where is the wisdom in differentiating day from night? Do the words of our prayers serve to mock our desire?

Of course not.

So then what purpose do these words serve? I would suggest that they are, in addition to being a petition to God, they are the first step in having our prayer answered. They are teaching us not that wisdom is found in being able to make this particular distinction but that wisdom resides in the *dynamic* of distinguishing.

The task of the wise is to distinguish. To differentiate. To contrast.

As in all things, in the matter of contrasts and distinctions, we look to God for guidance. For God Himself is the Master of the ability to distinguish and to create distinctions. We acknowledge as much when we mark the ebbing of the Sabbath by acknowledging God as the One who has, "...distinguished between the sacred and the profane, between Israel and the nations, between the seventh day and the six days of labor."

In our *bakasha* we confront these contrasts, elevated by God's implicit challenge that we not only recognize the superficiality of "differences" but we also engage in the powerful interplay of opposites on a deeper level. So we pray for wisdom, insight and discernment. We pray for the ability to distinguish; to separate. That our prayer comes during the *havdalah* service, the service which marks the boundary between the Sabbath and its opposite – the six days of labor only heightens the task at hand, as the very name of the service, "havdalah", means "to separate" and serves to emphasize the power of contrasts even more.

As Jews, our spiritual existence is an on-going process of contrasts and distinctions. When we speak of wisdom and understanding, we speak *almost exclusively* in terms of recognizing the significance of distinctions. In fact, we *cannot* gain understanding *but by* contrast.

Our Sages understood the significance of existence itself only in the context of the contrast between life in this world and in the world to come. "The world to come is to be compared to day, and this world is compared to night."

[Pesachim 2] "This world is compared to the eve of the Sabbath, and the world to come is compared to the Sabbath." [Avoda Zarah 3]

Within the larger, fundamental contrast of existence between this world and the world to come there existed a continual engagement with contrasts on a lesser level. "The world is to be compared to a ladder, this one going up and this one coming down." [Tanhuma Matot 9] "This world, the small can become the big, the big can become small." [Bereishit Rabbah 3:1]

Our Jewish sensibility finds much in common with a sensibility more often associated with Eastern, mystic influences. In the whole, the polar opposites are nestled together. Ying and yang. In Judaism, we see that in creation, *in and of itself*, rests the seed of destruction. Birth holds most fundamentally the eventual end, for all that is born dies. Although he was not a Jew, the poet T.S. Eliot captured the Jewish understanding exactly when he wrote, "In my beginning is my end."

Or, to use a very modern, technologically-savvy image: Existence – in its grand, universal sense as well as in its incremental, day to day experiences – is like an infinite series of contrasting binary realities, on-off, good-bad, light-dark, life-death, etc.

In the face of existence, whether understood poetically or in binary terms, we Jews are to live according to proscribed *mitzvot*, the commanded behaviors that define "holy" behavior. We would be justified in thinking that these God-directives, so concrete in their instruction, would serve almost as a divining rod to guide us in maintaining our balance on the narrow bridge that hangs between the contrast of existence, this world and the next. Isn't that what those who would demean Judaism as being "legalistic" would have us think? However, as we learn from Maimonides, far from relieving us from the need to dance with the shadows of contrasts, *mitzvot* place us at the very nexus where our need to distinguish is most profound.

The first, and most fundamental, of all *mitzvot* is the belief in One God. Maimonides refers to this *mitzvah* as "the foundation of foundations, [for] the pillar of all knowledge is to know that there is a prime being... and this knowledge is a positive commandment." Is there a person with religious sensibilities who could differ with this declaration, Jewish or not? Yet, Maimonides was too wise to believe that a straightforward, positive declaration would suffice to define *mitzvot* or our relationship with God. Maimonides also maintained the doctrine of negative attributes, *which denies all possibility of really knowing God.*

We do not often think of traditional Judaism existing within the terms of "existential crisis" but could a modern philosopher possibly articulate a more damning and awe-inspiring *co-existing* reality than the absolute truth that there is no greater guiding criterion for man than the Knowledge of God and the absolute truth that the Knowledge of God is not within the realm of human cognition?

"Are there two greater opposites than these?" Rabbi Soloveitchik asks. In the awed silence that must follow the Rav's questions, we must begin to understand Maimonides not simply as a man of cognition but also as a man of faith. As Rav suggests, "…negative cognition does not forfeit its status as cognition."

This assertion embraces the fundamental truth of contrasts. In this instance, that the absence of knowing is also a kind of knowing.

*Not*-knowing is knowing.

It is only by understanding and embracing a recognition of this contrast, and by extension, all others, that we find our way to our ultimate (though necessarily limited) understanding of complete truth. Again, using language not often associated with traditional Judaism, we must "surrender" to the recognition that we cannot *think* our way to meaning and understanding any more than the Buddhist monk could simply "answer" the question, What is the sound of one hand clapping? Although, by the same token, we must recognize that our ability to "not-think" is a condition of our thought process!

There is a deep truth here and it is the very truth that Moses prayed for and his petition was granted. "Indeed, we are all commanded to occupy ourselves with understanding in depth of these attributes, for they bring us to the love and fear of God." [Halakhic Man, p. 12]

To love and fear God.

Such an understanding of God demands that we confront many contrasts about our understanding of God and our world. For example, what are we to make of God's omniscience and our free will? How can the rational mind contemplate and fully grasp this contrast? If God has complete knowledge of all that was, is, and will be, how is it that man can operate as a free agent? (There are those who would suggest that God's knowledge is simply an "awareness" and not a determinant of the future. But others might suggest that when God is "aware" of the future, He has determined it. That such a thing is an essential aspect of God and His power.)

Man's free will is a fundamental truth of Jewish thought; we hold that God's absolute knowledge in no way *determines* whether man will do good or ill. But our assertion of that fundamental truth of Jewish thought casts us fully into the vortex of contrasts!

God is absolutely unchanging (we will discuss this fundamental reality of God, a reality encoded in the tetragammon, the four-letter name of God) and yet how could it be that He wasn't/isn't changed by His creation, the *constantly* changing universe? God is transcendent, ultimately beyond and removed from this world and yet He is imminent and ultimately near, standing at the gate.

Clearly, we ascribe many attributes and qualities to God and many of these stand in opposition to one another or, at the least, in opposition to other qualities and understandings we hold about the world and our place in it. The names by which we call God speak to this varied and contrasting reality. But one "identifier" speaks most clearly to His essence. *HaKadosh*. The Holy One. God's holiness defines all that we understand about God, all that we understand as truly meaningful, all that fully defines us as Jews – the Sabbath, the bond of the marriage contract, the candles we light on Hanukah.

The Hebrew *shoresh* for *kodesh*, K, D, Sh, suggests something that has been "set apart." That which is holy has been "set apart". But, of course, being "set apart" is meaningless unless we understand it as being set apart <u>from</u>. In other words, distinguished from. The Sabbath is holy because it is set apart from, different than, the six days of labor. The holiness of the marriage bond rests upon the unique, intimate, and "set apart" relationship enjoyed by that man and wife. The candles we light at Hanukah are holy because by the blessings we recite we distinguish them from any other candle whose purpose is merely to cast light.

To be holy is to be "set apart."

Holiness is the necessary result of a sharpened ability to distinguish between contrasts, to choose between right and wrong, good and evil, true and false, pure and impure, permissible and prohibited. "You shall be holy, for I am holy."

When a holy object is defiled, it loses that distinction, that contrast, with that which is not-holy.

Only God, the holy one, the one who is ultimately and completely "set apart" imbues holiness on the unchanging sameness of the everyday and the not-meaningful. God takes that sameness and by His very presence and existence, transforms it into "the other". Mircea Eliade, a twentieth-century theologian, taught that it was only by the immediate revelation of God that space or time becomes holy. Our world is, by definition, profane until God reveals His holiness. Then, that place where such a revelation takes place is "set apart", it becomes ultimately special and therefore, holy.

Eliade is an academic theologian. He is not a Jew and yet he is articulating something that we understand fundamentally. Doesn't he describe what happened to Jacob when he laid his head down to sleep and dreamed a dream of angels ascending and descending upon a ladder?

*"Surely the Lord is in this place, and I knew it not."*

*And he was afraid, and said, "How full of awe is this place! This is none other than the house of God, and this is the gate of heaven." And Jacob woke up early in the morning, and took the stone that he had put under his head, and set it up for a pillar, and poured oil upon the top of it. And he called the name of that place, Beth El...*

Breishit 28:16-19

Jacob was in a place "no different from any other place" except perhaps by its physical characteristics until God revealed Himself to <u>be there</u> in that place, distinguishing it and setting apart from "any other place." For this now became the place where God revealed Himself. It was now Holy.

God is absolutely Holy because He is set apart from everything. He is absolutely and fundamentally unique. He is separated from the earth in that He is not made of matter; He is separated from time in that He is everlasting, eternal. He has no beginning and no end; He is also separated from the Heavens in that He has no form.

To be set apart, to be *in contrast to*, is to be holy. Israel's holiness is the direct consequence of her adherence to *mitzvot*. "As it is written, 'And be holy unto your God'; when you observe the commandments, you are holy, and the fear of you lies upon the idolaters. But if you part from the commandments and commit sins, you forthwith become profaned.'"

The *mitzvot* call Israel apart. When we part with them, we make ourselves *like* the other nations. There is no distinction. There is no contrast. There is no holiness. We make ourselves not-holy, or profane.

Contrasts are fundamental to the essence of God and holiness so it should come as no surprise that contrasts dominate so many of the *mitzvot*, principles and observances of Judaism as well. Indeed, in order to get a sense of the whole one needs to gather the shards of contrasts through the prism of experience.

Tisha B'Av, the saddest of all days in the Jewish liturgical year, commemorates national calamity and destruction. Yet, it is described in *Eicha* as a *moed*, a festival. The lesson is clear, in dejection resides joy.

The destruction of the Temples sent us into the tragedy of our *Galut*. Our homeless wanderings were hard for us. We cried with the Psalmist that we would never forget Jerusalem. Yet our *Galut* was like the fire that hardened and molded us. We found meaning in our wanderings, meaning that could only be understood through the perspective of *G'ulah* – redemption.

There was nobility in our personal and communal suffering, nobility that could only be embraced with our understanding of the redemption to come. The Midrash states: "Before the birth of the first oppressors of the Jewish people, the final redeemer was born."

Can you grasp the complete brilliance of this understanding! If not, then the fullness of meaning will always elude you. Tragedy does not exist without joy. Bitterness and want, without fulfillment. Even as Joseph was being sold as a slave to Potipher in Egypt, setting in motion a long and bitter *Galut*, God was planting the seeds of the coming *G'ulah* by arranging the union of Yehuda and Tamar.

Only by placing the contrasting pieces in the puzzle is it possible to begin to understand His ways. Moshe Rabbeinu asked God to reveal His face to him. What was God's response? "You will see My back, but not My face."

Where is the logic of this answer? Moses is asking to be made aware of God's plan for history, even that which appears inexplicable and incomprehensible as it occurs. God's response makes clear that, while on the face of things events seem senseless and erratic, the long arc of history, with its conflicts and contrasts nestled together, is one of meaning.

No *Galut* without *G'ulah*.

The God who exiles His people, who has allowed the cities of Israel to become desolate, will bring His people back. And, while they live in the land of their enemies, He will accompany them Himself.

The people Israel will always know *G'ulah*, even in the depths of *Galut*.

TIME –

Eliade, in defining sacrality as a "break with the ordinary", as "otherness" spoke of both sacred space and sacred time. While sacred space is vital to Jewish existence – from Jacob's Beth-El to Jerusalem – it is sacred time that is most fundamental to our sense of who we are.

Interwoven into the fabric of Jewish existence are strands of the past, the challenge of the present, and the hope of the future. To be Jewish means to stand in this ever-dangerous current of time and, in the midst of destruction and *Galut*, to be able to embrace the hope of *G'ulah*. It is, in short, a completely irrational stance, one that seems better suited for drowning than for redemption.

Despite the common perception as being legalistic, we Jews are best understood when we are seen as being poetic, irrational and embracing that which is beyond embrace. How could it be otherwise? Our existence depends entirely upon Him who is beyond comprehension, on grasping for Him who cannot be grasped, on touching that which cannot be touched.

In the Book of Job, a righteous man was deliberately beset with tragedy as a way to demonstrate his faith in God. Through each and every tragedy – and these were horrific tragedies that none of us should ever have to endure - Job maintained his faith in God. However, there finally reached a point when Job cried out to God that he wanted to know exactly what was happening, and he wanted to know directly from God. He wanted a "witness".

In other words, like Moses, he wanted to have a "face to face" with God.

God's response? "Where were you when the foundations of the earth were laid?" and, "If you cannot run with men, how do you expect to run with stallions?" God responds with righteous indignation.

Scholars have long debated the "meaning" of the Book of Job, God's role in Job's suffering and His responses to Job's plea for understanding. Certainly, God's answers did not actually "answer" any of Job's questions. One might argue that they didn't even *address* the questions.

Yet, Job's response to them was a reaffirmed faith.

In the face of incomprehensibility, faith?

Absolutely. For the details of God's response was not the issue. What did Job care about words? *That* God responded was all that was required. For God's response affirmed His existence and, so long as God exists, then *everything* has meaning. Even *Galut*.

Dostoevski, the great Russian writer, said that in the absence of God, "...murder is no more than a leaf falling in the forest." However, the simple fact of God's existence, which cannot help but appear irrational to our eyes, is sufficient to make meaningful that which appears absurd or meaningless.

Our existence depends upon God. Incomprehensible God. Unattainable God. The mere fact of God's existence is what shimmers unity into the contrasts.

All of life is taken up with the interplay of contrasts. As Solomon teaches us in *Kohelet*:

To everything is a season...

A time for every experience under heaven.

A time for being born, and a time for dying.

A time for planting and a time for uprooting the planted.

A time for slaying and time for healing.

A time for tearing down and a time for building up.

A time for weeping and a time for laughing.

A time for wailing and a time for dancing.

A time for throwing stones and a time for gathering stones together.

A time for embracing and a time for shunning embraces.

A time for seeking and a time for losing.

A time for keeping and a time for discarding.

A time for ripping and time for sewing.

A time for silence and a time for speaking.

A time for loving and a time for hating.

A time for war and a time for peace.

When one has observed a time for each of these things, he will find that he has lived a life indeed.

It is in the context of time that we understand God as being wholly and utterly "other" and most sacred. Completely and absolutely Holy.

When God called Moses to approach the Pharaoh and demand that he free the enslaved Jews, Moses balked. He asked God, "Who shall I say sent me?" In response to this question, God identified himself by His sacred name, the tetragammon.

The conventional translation of God's sacred name, the tetragammon, is "I am who I am." I hold that this translation falls short, sapping the power of God's name of its fundamental, identifying power. The tetragammon, the letters of which I would not even write here out of utter respect, comes from a family of words that have to do with "being," with existence itself. Therefore, a more accurate translation of God's name might be, "I am as I always will be."

God's name, therefore, speaks to His essential nature. Unlike those of us who exist in time, whose physical, intellectual, psychological and spiritual natures are changing minute by minute, even second by second, as we accrue more and more experience, God's nature is unchanging. God is unchanging. In other words, He exists outside the current of time. It is *not* that God is immortal, which would suggest that He simply lives from the beginning to the end. God actually <u>exists outside the parameters of time</u>.

This fundamental reality about God makes the central truth of the Passover – that God, beyond the bounds of time, would actually *enter* the flow of history to free the Jews – that much starker in its contrasts. Indeed, time is at the heart of the Jewish narrative and the sanctity of time is fundamental to who we are as a people. It is also in sacred time that we discover ever more contrasts.

PESACH, TIMLESSNESS AND TIME –

How do we confront the greatest paradox of historical time, that the God who is beyond time should enter history, imbue it with His presence, to liberate Israel from bondage? That sacred time exists in Judaism, as it does in all other belief systems, is not – in and of itself – of particular note. However, the paradox, the contrast, of timelessness not simply "touching time" as Eliade might suggest but entering into its very essence is awe inspiring.

From this awesome foundation, Pesach occupies a liturgical and ritual place that very likely encompasses a wider variety of contrasting experiences and observances than any other day in the Jewish liturgical year. Pesach, the "time of our redemption" calls upon us first and foremost to remember the time of our enslavement. "We were slaves to Pharaoh in the land of Egypt. Now we are free."

Only the enslaved truly understand freedom and only the free truly grasp bondage.

At the Seder, we sit garbed in a *kitel*, the death shroud. What is the logic of this? That we dress as if dead at the very moment we celebrate our great liberation? But the whiteness of the garment speaks to more than death. The white color of the *kitel* symbolizes purity, joy and happiness.

In the very clothes we wear to the Seder, we cloak ourselves in the essential paradox of death – that it is bracketed by unknowable darkness on either side.

During the Seder, we dip our green herb twice. The first time, as the Sh'la explains, as a remembrance of the *G'ulah*, the redemption, reminiscent of the "hyssop, dipped in the blood that is in the basin, touched on the lintel and the two side posts," which kept the first-born of the Israelites safe during that terrible night when the Angel of Death passed over the land of the Egyptians. The second time we dip, we dip in remembrance of the *Galut*, the dispersion which began with the sale of Joseph to the caravan of traders, and the dipping of his coat of many colors in the blood.

The T'zlach explained that the green vegetables eaten with the first dipping symbolize nature, peace and tranquility. The feeling of a free man. The *maror*, dipped into the *charoset* calls to mind the mortar and the stuff of our slavery.

Freedom and slavery, liberation and bondage, the contrasts of Pesach are profound and ever-present in the rituals associated with the holiday. It is customary to eat the egg from the Seder plate at the beginning of the Seder meal. There are those who explain the symbolism of the egg to represent the *korban chagigah*, an expression of a happy, family-oriented celebration. For others, the egg is a symbol of mourning. Its place of honor on the Seder table is to remind us of the destruction of the Temple and our inability to fully celebrate the Pesach until it is rebuilt.

This connection between the tragedy of the Temple's destruction and our liberation is further highlighted when we note that Tisha B'Av is observed on whatever day of the week the first day of Pesach is celebrated. Freedom and destruction. Liberation and enslavement. *G'ulah* and *Galut*.

Like the egg, the symbol of our humiliation and pain can be elevated to symbolize our greatest aspirations and joy. Recall that the Western Wall, the Kotel, was left standing by Titus, the Roman general, not as a monument to our glory but as a reminder of Rome's glory; an artifact meant to demean and humiliate us.

After all, of the Second Temple, this one piece of the outermost wall was allowed to remain standing. To Titus, that was a more powerful statement about the relative weakness of the Jews than to have completely razed every last stone of the Temple and its environs. So what did we do? We made that fragment of our former glory the focal point of our hopes and dreams. The Wailing Wall, where we went to weep and to pray, remembering what was – and what *would once again be*.

So it was that when God instructed Moses to "slaughter the Paschal sacrifice" Moses hesitated. "Master of the World, how can I slaughter it? Don't you know that the lamb is the god of the Egyptians?" God responded to Moses' concern by swearing that the Israelites, "...would not leave here until the god of the Egyptians is slaughtered in front of their eyes."

On that terrible night, what had been a symbol of Egyptian idolatry became a symbol of sanctity and holiness to the Israelites. For the blood of that unblemished lamb was the sign that guarded the houses of the Israelites and kept watch over the sleeping first born sons. Essential to the power of understanding contrasts is the understanding that it is within the capacity of each of us to transform the lowliest into the loftiest; that each of us, by the grace of God, can make the profane sacred.

Perhaps few things make clear this ability to transform, to perform *t'shuvah*, than the *parah adumah*, the red heifer. This *parah* has the ability to "repair" the essence of our greatest spiritual bankruptcy – the golden calf. Inherent within the nature of the *parah adumah* is the greatest contrast of all – its ability to make pure the impure and to contaminate the pure. Perhaps this is the reason that Pesach is preceded by Shabbat Parah – to remind us that the "forty-nine levels of impurity" are transferred and uplifted to the "forty-nine levels of Torah."

Rabbi Nehemiah cited in the Talmud teaches [Sanhedrin 70a] regarding the forbidden tree from which Adam ate, "it was the fig tree whereby they transgressed and whereby they were taught to make amends," as it is written, "And they sewed fig leaves together." Here, Rabbi Nehemiah teaches that the very source of sinfulness was also the means of repentance and redemption.

The Pesach Seder is "anchored" by the drinking of the four cups of wine, each of which is associated to a specific *mitzvah* of the Seder. The Talmud *Yerushalmi* cites four reasons for the *mitzvah* of the Four Cups. The first associates the four cups with the four expressions of redemption found in *Shemot*.

*V'hotzeti*: I will take you out from under the burdens of Egypt.

*V'hitzalti*: I will save you from their work.

*V'gaalti*: I will redeem you with a strong arm and great judgments.

*V'lakachti*: I will take you unto Me for a nation.

While each of these speaks to the power and magnificence of God in liberating Israel from bondage there are other explanations as well. For example, there are the four times when cups are mentioned in the dream of Pharaoh's butler. "And Pharaoh's cup was in my hand; and I took the grapes, and pressed them into Pharaoh's cup, and I gave the cup into Pharaoh's hand… and you shall give Pharaoh's cup into his hand." This explanation utilizes the power of contrasts in that we take the "cup" of our oppressor, the Pharaoh, and rather than a symbol of our oppression it becomes a symbol of the greatness of God and our own liberation.

The other explanation focuses on the four regional powers who dominated and tormented the Jewish nation in ancient times. Kasdim, Madai, Yavan, and Edom. We recall these oppressors when we recite *Shfoch Chamatecha* when we stand by the open door that invites Elijah into our midst. We pray for God to, "pour out His wrath upon the nations that know you not."

Through this connection to our oppressors and our liberation, the contrasting symbols of the four cups of wine create a powerful image of our redemption – both at the time of our slavery in Egypt and in the future. Though there are always those who would seek to oppress us, God is our salvation and we will be redeemed.

So, while on the surface it seems that the Talmud *Yerushalmi* has presented us with four very different reasons for the ritual of the Four Cups, in fact our deeper insight makes clear that each of these reasons stands as a contrasting facet on the same "diamond." We have the four expressions of redemption in balance with the four cups of Pharaoh, and the four oppressors in opposition to the four cups of consolation.

How can a Jew who participates in this magnificent ritual fail to recognize – and find consolation in – God's redemption and our survival from the tyranny and oppression from the Pharaohs who will always rise up to harm us. We noted that the *Shfoch Chamatecha* is recited when we open the door to invite Elijah into our presence. We pray for God to bring His wrath upon the nations at the very moment when we are contemplating our ultimate redemption.

It is impossible to fully comprehend the depth of the misery and humiliation of slavery and oppression save for in contrast to God's redemption. So too, we cannot fully contemplate our ultimate redemption but by contrasting it with the depths of our despair.

God ensures that the Israelites in Egypt experienced the fullness of the contrast between their humiliation and their coming redemption when He instructed Moshe to tell the Israelites, "*Daber na b'oznei ha'am* – "And let every man ask of his neighbor, and every woman of her neighbor, jewels of silver and jewels of gold."

As Rashi explains, the "*na*" in this expression is of great significance. In Hebrew, this small word expresses something akin to a polite request. "Please." Rashi understands the verse to be saying, "Please keep on reminding them, so that the righteous man, Abraham, should not say: 'And they shall enslave them and they shall afflict them.'" In his teaching, Rashi reminds us that God's revelation to Abraham was that his children would be enslaved in a strange land for many, many years but that they would also experience redemption and security – *ve'achrei ken yetzu birchush gadol.*

Leaving Egypt with jewels was not the impulsive action of runaway slaves. It was not akin to the looting we sometimes see when cities and towns experience violent upheaval. God forbid! Leaving Egypt with the jewels of their oppressors was an act of deliberation. It fulfilled the predetermined Divine plan. This was an act of Divine retribution and justice.

The Jew of *Galut* cannot survive without the promise of *G'ulah*. The Midrash relates that God showed Abraham four elements of Jewish existence: *Gehenom* and *Galut*, the Revelation of Torah and the Temple. In doing so, God assured Abraham that Jews will exist when they recognize the contrasts of their existence.

We find in the conclusion of *Breishit* the seeds of the *Galut* to come. Jacob, the last Patriarch, eagerly anticipates his reunion with Joseph, his favored son, yet God sees fit to "reassure" Jacob before his journey. "I am God, the God of thy father; fear not to go down to Egypt."

Fear going down to Egypt? Jacob had expressed no such trepidation! Quite the opposite. He had declared clearly that, "I will go and see him before I die."

Jacob's desire to see Joseph, whom he had not seen for over two decades and for whom he had mourned inconsolably, was not tempered by any trepidation. And yet, God instructed him not to fear.

Why?

According to Rashi, Jacob was, "...distressed because he had been obligated to leave the homeland." Despite the fact that he knew that he was going to a land of plenty, where his beloved son was the vice-regent, he did not want to leave because he knew that his departure would usher in the *Galut*. He knew that he was going to Egypt to fulfill the ancient prophecy given to his forefathers regarding the period of bondage and suffering. Perhaps worse, how could he know that his descendents would ever *want* to return to the Promised Land?

Jacob, the archetypal wrestler, found himself wrestling with the contrasting forces of *Galut* and *G'ulah*. How could he know that his descendents would not be absorbed in the larger, richer, more powerful Egyptian nation? Only in the Land of Israel could the unique Jewish spark be nurtured and protected through the ages.

And so, God reassured him. "Fear not, for there I shall make of thee a great nation."

In doing so, God made clear to Jacob that which is beyond our comprehension – that *Galut* and *G'ulah* are intrinsically and eternally wedded. And what is the "bond" that holds these two extreme forces in a singular orbit? God Himself. "I will go to Egypt with you, and I will also bring you back again. As the Mechilta notes, the Israelites never descended to *Galut* without God accompanying them nor did they ever return with God ascending with them.

In this truth do we glimpse the power of contrasts. For in addressing them, we glimpse the power of God.

Our sages teach us that, "*Matchil bignut u'msayem bishevach*; we begin with shame and conclude with the praise." [Pesachim 116a] This then is the ultimate contrast of the Passover narrative and the message of the Haggadah – we begin with shame and end with praise. Our ritual weds the contrasting poles of our experience in being enslaved and then being redeemed.

Struggling to encompass these two counterweights has, in the view of Rabbi Soloveitchik, been the "experience which molded the moral quality of the Jewish people for all time."

Just as an individual finds his best characteristics and qualities molded by the adversity he faces, the Jewish people, called to holiness by God, could only begin to *be* holy because of the experience of being enslaved.

Egypt taught us to be ethical. In the deepest sense, it taught us what it means to be a Jew. And not because we suffered. If we look upon the experience of our slavery and saw *only* our own suffering and redemption we will miss the essential lesson of our experience. Because we have suffered *we are able to appreciate the suffering of others*. That is the holiness that our experience grants us.

"Love the stranger, for you were strangers too, in the land of Egypt."

The Torah and our experiences teach us compassion and sympathy for the oppressed and underprivileged in society by reminding us of our former state of helplessness. How many of those who were formerly low become haughty and seek to forget that experience? For them, their shame is a cause for secretiveness. Such people do not understand the transformative nature of contrasts. For it is only by being brought low that one can truly rise high.

As Jews, we embrace our suffering – not because there is any inherent benefit to suffering as such but because it is our suffering that has opened our eyes to the suffering of others; our suffering which allows us to fully appreciate the gift of freedom; our *galut* which allows us to understand and to grasp our *g'ulah*.

Our experience of *Galut* refines our sense of right and wrong. "You shall not pervert the justice due to a stranger or to the fatherless; nor take a widow's garment in pawn."

Why not?

Throughout the world, it too often seems that the very *reason* that governments exist is to allow the powerful to do exactly this, to pervert justice and to take advantage of the vulnerable. So, why not the Jews? Because God reminds us, "Remember that you were a slave in Egypt, and the Lord your God redeemed you; therefore, I command you to observe this commandment."

We are exhorted *thirty-six times* in the Torah to treat the stranger with kindness. Why? *Ki gerim heitem beeertz mitzrayim* – because you were strangers too, in the land of Egypt. God makes clear that it has been our experience of these contrasts that teaches us the lesson of mercy, of *rachmanus*. It is not arbitrary. No more than God "justifying" the Ten Commandments by the preamble, "And God spoke all these words, saying: "I am the Lord your God, who brought you out of the land of Egypt, out of the house of bondage."

*Galut* allows us the privilege and the blessing of *G'ulah*!

The Torah teaches us not to work the servant "with rigor." That is, not to assign the *eved* work that would "break him" – *lo tirde bo befarech*. Note, this exhortation presumes that we Jews *are in the position* to have servants at our command. In other words, that we are enjoying some aspect of real *g'ulah*. It is in this context that we are commanded *not* to give our servant work that would "break him." The Hebrew word, *befarech*, appears only two other times in the Torah and both these times in the context of the backbreaking tasks assigned to the Israelites in Egypt.

*Befarech*! To the Jew, this term has deep power. Only those of us who suffered degradation, humiliation, and abuse can fully – and genuinely – guarantee the rights and dignity of the servant.

The contrast of master and slave has taught us the value of mercy and kindness. The two poles, contrasts, that cannot be wed by human understanding or effort, is made whole by God. "I am the Lord who brought you out of Egypt to be your God…"

It is only by the *experience* of want that one is able to truly appreciate the grace of being able to be giving.

## THE SEDER

The Seder itself, with its many rituals, is a model of contrast experience. Even as we are free men, we are slaves. *Avadeem hayeenu*. We were slaves. *Ata b'nei horin*. Now we are free. We recline at our seats in a posture symbolic of our liberation and freedom as we recall the humiliations of our slavery. Even as we eat *matzah*, symbol of our redemption, we eat the *maror*, the bitter herb, symbol of our enslavement.

The Seder revolves around questions and paradoxes. We are instructed to create an environment which will engage the youngest present so that they will become engaged in the powerful interplay of contrasts.

*Mah nishtana*? Why is this night different? From its outset, the Seder points us to the nexus of the fundamental contrast in Jewish life – between slave and free man. In doing so, we turn our children's attention to God, the mystery presence who makes these contrasts meaningful.

For those of us who are no longer young, the Seder challenges us to confront the dilemma of whether we can ever truly come to grips with life's contrasts. Is it really possible to appreciate the point at which we are no longer enslaved but are indeed free? What does it mean to be free in our world? Or in the context of an all-knowing God? Do we possess the capacities to wear the *kitel* while at the same time recognizing our angelic qualities while at the same time contemplating our finite state – the breath of God and the dust of the earth?

Pesach and the Seder teach us many contrasts and also the lesson that the unifying power that brings the paradoxical opposites into unity is none other than God Himself. Perhaps this was never more evident than a long ago Seder in the Bergen Belsen Concentration Camp.

Imagine the scene. Could any of us imagine a more frightening place for a Seder? Could there have been a deeper sense of *Galut* than what those Jews felt? Imagine the mood as the Rabbi of Bluzhov sat at the head of the modest Seder table, surrounded by a group of young children and a handful of adults. He invited the youngest to ask the Four Questions. In a sweet, child-like voice, he began the familiar melody. "Why is this night different from all other nights? On all other nights, we eat either bread or matzah; but on this night, we eat only matzah…"

As is customary, the rabbi began to explain the meaning of the Passover. But on that Seder night in Bergen Belsen, the ancient questions of the Haggadah could not help but have deeper meaning.

"Night," the rabbi said, "means exiles, darkness, suffering. Morning means light, hope, redemption. Why is this night different from all other nights? Why is this suffering different from all the previous sufferings of the Jewish people?"

Rabbi Israel Spira continued, "For on all other nights we eat either bread or matzah, but tonight only matzah. Bread is leavened; it has height. Matzah is unleavened and is totally flat. During our previous nights in exile, we had moments of bread, of creativity, and light, and moments of matzah, of suffering and despair. But tonight, we experience our greatest suffering. Tonight, we have only matzah. We have no moments of relief... But do not despair, my young friends."

With that powerful introduction, the rabbi continued in a strong voice, a voice filled with faith and hope.

"For this is also the beginning of our redemption. We are slaves who served Pharaoh in Egypt. Slaves in Hebrew is *Avadim*; the Hebrew letters of the word *Avadim* form an acronym for the Hebrew phrase, "David, the son of Jesse, your servant, your Messiah." The rabbi's eyes were alight with the fire of hope, of *G'ulah*. Even in that most horrible of *Galuyot*, his soul was alight with *G'ulah*. "Do you see, my children? Even in our state of slavery, we find intimation of our eventual freedom through the coming of the Messiah.

"We, who are witnessing the darkest night in history, the lowest moment of civilization, will also witness the great light of redemption, for before the great light there must be a long night..."

The Seder concluded. As the children returned to their barracks, slaves of a modern Pharaoh amidst a desert of mankind, they were certain that they could hear the sounds of the Messiah's footsteps echoing in their own, in the blood-soaked gravel of Bergen Belsen.

THE DAYS OF AWE; ROSH HASHANAH AND YOM KIPPUR –

Pesach is the canvas of our greatest historical and ritual contrasts. It is the terrible Egyptian *Galut* that informs our embrace of the gift of *G'ulah*. It is the timelessness of God entering time-intensive history that highlights the power of that fundamental contrast. Our liturgical calendar is filled with other holidays that are defined by contrasts – as they all must be if they are truly "holy days" for we have come to understand that "holiness" in some guise means to wed the polar contrasts that confront us.

Rosh HaShanah and Yom Kippur are the "bookends" that bracket the fearful and uplifting ten days of awe. Each day carries the weight of a great, eternal theme. Rosh HaShanah is *Yom HaDin*, the Day of Judgment and Justice. Yom Kippur is *Yom HaRachamim*, the Day of Love, Compassion and Forgiveness.

*Din* – judgment, harsh demanding, unyielding.

*Rachmanus* – righteousness, love, patient, gentle, forbearing.

Together, they define the High Holidays. Both are attributes we associate with God and both infuse each and every day of our lives. These two themes represent powerful contrasts in life. We would each love to imagine a utopian life in which *only* justice and mercy exists. Yet such a world would be frightfully unfulfilling and sadly without meaning. For it is the contrasts that give meaning to life.

The Greek philosopher, Plato, taught a more eloquent version of "the grass is always greener on the other side of the fence." He taught that the basic values of human life are never fully appreciated during one's lifetime or while in possession of them. In other words, "you never know what you've got until you've lost it."

The young and healthy cannot possibly appreciate their youthfulness and good health. That is left to the aged and the infirm. Those who know only comfort could not be expected to appreciate the real joy of their comfort. True want is required first.

Many parents do their children a disservice by simply buying their children whatever they want. The bicycle that is *earned* is always appreciated more than the one that is *received*.

How many Americans, fairly oblivious to the gifts that come naturally to citizens of this country, find themselves in a foreign land and sigh to themselves, "There's no place like America." For that matter, how many people find themselves away from home only to utter those most powerful words, "There's no place like home"? It is only by *being someplace else* that we fully appreciate the place we are.

Men do not argue for peace during times of quiet and prosperity. They long for peace during times of war and upheaval. It is only when death is imminent that we long for life. Isn't this really the source of the much ballyhooed "mid-life crisis"? It is only when we feel that we can no longer *be* young that we behave in a way that grotesquely mimics being young again.

We want that which we do not have.

Rabbi Soloveitchik suggests that this "philosophy of contrasts" is not true only in the mundane, everyday world of health, home and politics. It also holds "for the highest value in man's life – awareness of God." Just as illness brings us an understanding of health and age an appreciation of youth, our distance from God serves to reawaken in us His significance.

Jewish history is replete with our suffering, made more terrible because of our wrong-headedness in distancing ourselves from God. Our history and destiny necessitated the cruelties of our enslavement, the Crusades and blood libels, even the horror of the *Shoah* in order to bring us to our sense of basic theology. For so many, it is not until they stand in the shadow of death that they utter the words, *Baruch atah Hashem* and then, only with the closing *Dayan Emet*, God is the righteous Judge.

Soloveitchik sees sin as the prism through which man repents. Think of the brilliance of this seemingly contradictory perspective – that it is only through sin that one can perform true *t'shuvah*. It is such an obvious – and yet elusive – truth. *T'shuvah* is, in fact, meaningless *but* in the presence of sin. The halachic concept of *t'shuvah* vouchsafes us the revelation that there are new values accessible to us from the reality of our natures, from *where we are*.

For we do not live in the optative world, the world of "would that it were." We exist in the world as it is, a world desperate for *tikkun*. We do not live in a utopia. After all, the name "utopia" means, quite literally, "no place." We live in the reality of time, of sin, of sickness and persecution. Life would be unbearable as such if not for the contrast that these very realities allow us to grasp holiness, forgiveness, and peace.

The Talmud teaches that there even exists an element of contrast in man's understanding of God before and after he sins. *Hashem, Hahem k'El Rachum Vichanun.* "I am the Lord before man sins, and I am the Lord after man sins."

That God is God before and after man sins should come as no surprise. God is as He always will be. However, it is man who changes. And man when he sins is more able to measure the grace of holiness and forgiveness.

That God is God as the sun sets on *erev Rosh HaShanah* and again at the close of *ne'elah* on Yom Kippur should surprise no one. It is man who changes during those ten days filled with awe.

We are called before the throne of God. We are confronted by our sins – and therefore made ready to delight in repentance and forgiveness. *Rosh HaShanah*, day of judgment, instills new hope for a new beginning, a fresh start and an optimistic future.

In the most ancient of the High Holiday liturgy, *Avinu Malkeinu* (mentioned in the Talmud Tanith 25b as the prayer of Rabbi Akiva on a fast-day), we acknowledge that "we have no King but Thee" and we beseech God to "deal kindly with us for the sake of Thy Name." Yet, we also invoke those "who were slain for Thy Holy Name," and those who went through fire and water "for the sanctification of Thy Name." We recall the "spilt blood of Thy servants" and pray for God's revenge.

That these contrasting appeals should appear in a single prayer is overwhelming. That we should approach God *in this prayer* as both Father and King speaks to the inherent contrasts. We approach God as a kind, merciful and loving being while *at the same time* approach Him as a strict, unforgiving powerful judge and ruler.

Of course, we acknowledge that contrasts are not only inherent in God's nature, in life and the world, but in our very identity as a people as well. The Jewish people are one, great contrast.

We are the children not of Jacob but of Avraham, who was named Avraham because he stood on one side of the river while everyone else in the world stood on the other side. He stood in faith and opposition! Have we not been in that selfsame position throughout history? Have we not borne out the prophesy that we would be an *am levadad yishkon* – a lone and lonely nation?

Isaac was alone at Moriah, even as the world looked on. Jacob too was alone as he wrestled with an angel of God. And so it has gone through the generations even to today. The children of Avraham, Isaac, and Jacob remain "set apart" and alone amidst a cruel and immoral world. And what is it that sets us apart?

God's call to holiness.

During the High Holidays, *hayom harat olam* – a new world is born; the destiny of each of us is decided anew. *Im ke'vanim im ka'avadim.* Some will go forth as children of our heavenly Father, coaxed by *rachamim* and tenderness. Others will walk fearlessly, driven to obey the will of the divine King as His servants, challenged by ideals of justice. But none will be unchanged. We will each be forged in the fires of contrast, formed a new person who is resolved to answer to God – as Father or as King.

We implore God in the fullness of these contrasts for a blessed New Year. *Avinu Malkeinu.*

*Im ke'vanim, rachamenu ke'rachem av al banim v'im ka'avadim, lecha enenu teluyot ad she'techanenu ve'totzi la'or mishpateinu.* If we be like children to Thee, then treat us lovingly, as befits a Father; if we be servants to Thee, O Divine King, we look to Thee for a judgment as clear and as shining as light itself.

## ROSH CHODESH, THE MYSTERY OF THE NEW MOON –

When Titus of Rome destroyed the Second Temple in 70 c.e. he built a triumphal arch in Rome to mark his victory. He decorated the arch with reliefs of the holy vessels used in the Temple, including the seven-branched menorah. He issued coins inscribed with the words, *Judea Capta* and *Judea Devicta* ("Judea is captured" and "Judea is vanquished.")

What self-respecting Jew would pass under this arch? It stood as an artifact to our utter humiliation. However, much as we "rewrote" his intention regarding the remnants of the Temple serving as a constant reminder of our degradation and humiliation, when Israel was once again a nation amongst nations, the government chose the seven-branched menorah as its national symbol, elevating that which was used to humiliate us to a position of honor.

Rather than a symbol of being vanquished, it became a symbol of rebirth and strength. Just as the symbol of the menorah was transformed, so too have we been continually transformed from *avdut* to *cherut*, from *yagon* (agony) to *simcha* (joy) and from *afeila* (the darkness of the past) to *ohr gadol* (the great light of the future). Being Jewish means to be continually transformed, to cling to hope, to recognize in the contrasts of life the redemption to come.

Has our history justified our optimism? Is our hope ever rational? Certainly, when the humiliated survivors of the *Shoah* staggered out from the gates of Auschwitz it would have been perceived as sheer madness to be hopeful. Yet, when hundreds of thousands entered the port of Haifa to rebuild our homeland, our hope was justified.

Was hope a rational perspective when the rag-tag army of volunteers and survivors faced the armed forces of the Arab states, comprised of populations forty times the population of the budding Jewish state? And yet...

And yet...

Over and over again in our history, our narrative has appeared most bleak only to have God rewrite a new beginning for us. In the Torah, there are two beginnings, the textual one that begins the narrative of creation: In the beginning, God created... and the second, found in *parashat Bo*: "This month shall be the head month to you. It shall be the first month of the year."

Rashi argued that it was this second beginning that should have marked the beginning of *Breishit* because, unlike the "first" beginning, this second one teaches us that creation is ongoing. There is constant renewal and, with constant renewal, constant reason for hope.

This on-going dynamic of change and rebirth finds its natural symbol in the phases of the moon. As Jews, our celebration of the New Moon – *Rosh Chodesh* – is a singular kind of celebration. It stands apart from all other celebrations in the Jewish year – Shabbat and *yamim tovim*.

On its face, *Rosh Chodesh* is an uneventful and inauspicious day. There are no restrictions on labor, no meaningful or practical observance demanded. Its significance and importance is, in effect, hidden.

There is a sense of *tzniut*, modesty, inherent in *Rosh Chodesh*. There is a feminine quality to it. Its mystery is subtle and its sanctity must be sought out, as with the most significant principles, themes, and elements of Judaism.

In so many ways, *Rosh Chodesh*, with its focus on the constantly transforming and transformed moon, provides the most fitting allegory for our beliefs and practices. Rabbi Soloveitchik suggests that while Shabbat and the other *Yomim Tovim* derive their sanctity and significance from specific historical or religious events and eras – whether Creation, Revelation or the Exodus from Egypt, the power of *Rosh Chodesh* emanates from the Jewish sense and belief in renewal.

*Rosh Chodesh* represents eternal faith in redemption, in the shining light yet to come. For *Rosh Chodesh*, the New Month, occurs when the new moon "appears" in the sky. That is, when there is no visible moon at all. There is darkness. We celebrate that darkness because of our knowledge that change is intrinsic to the world and that light will surely follow.

*Rosh Chodesh* is a statement, a declaration of the eternal optimist. It is the song of the Jew. It is the new song we sing.

The Talmud observes that Jews utilize a lunar calendar while the nations of the world rely on a solar calendar. The Sfat Emet says that this is because the nations of the world can only function and exist when conditions are favorable and their environment is sunny. When the sun sets, so do their empires. Jews, on the other hand, live and thrive even in the darkness. Even when we are humiliated and persecuted, just as the moon lights the world even in the thickest darkness, we survive. We thrive.

We find *G'ulah* even in *Galut.*

How else to understand that Seder in Bergen Belsen? The nations of the world would have said that it was pointless to continue the ritual of the Seder. "Just look, all around us all is lost." But not the Jews. The old Jews in Poland who took God to trial and found him guilty for "crimes against humanity" did not wrap themselves in sack cloth and bemoan the end of the world. Rather, they saw that, at the conclusion of the trial, the sun was rising.

"Nu, *rabbotai,* it's time to daven *shacharis.*"

Even should we hold God guilty, we would pray to God and praise Him. Ultimately, the contrasts in the world, and our understanding, negotiation, and reconciliation of them – in other words, the process of "becoming holy" and being fully Jewish – rely upon God.

God, who exists outside of all and therefore encompasses all, is all contrasts. By contemplating these contrasts, we glimpse something of the power of God's nature and, in doing so, become a little bit more holy.

# In Our Hearts and In the World

## Honesty and Ethics in Jewish Law and Tradition

## What Harm?

hat harm?

What harm in the student altering an answer on an exam in order to avoid a failing grade? Or copying a couple of paragraphs from an article in order to complete an assignment?

What harm?

Would the world really stop spinning on its axis if such minor infractions were tolerated? After all, the fact of the matter is that such infractions occur *each and every day*. Is the world really any worse off?

What harm is there in a small bit of deception – a *small* lie – if no one gets hurt in the process?

Such a *laissez faire* attitude might carry the day amongst those for whom honesty and dishonesty are not character traits but tolerable – and equally allowable – strategies for getting ahead in the world; to be employed as the situation dictates and used for advantage.

But there is a reason that "*laissez faire*" is a language other than Hebrew. Jewish law is clear in the matter of such ethical dishonesty: engaging in any form of intellectual dishonesty, including cheating on exams, plagiarizing, is strictly forbidden. It is non-negotiable. Such unethical behavior is not just a matter of "situational ethics"; it constitutes *genevat da'at*, which means, literally, "theft of the mind" but is more commonly understood to be "misrepresentation" – a much more global and all-encompassing category.

A *gonev da'at* is one who intentionally misleads or gives a false impression through his words or deeds. It does not matter if "no one is harmed" or if the dishonesty was not actually witnessed by one's fellow. It is always and absolutely wrong. It is a matter of Torah, for the Torah demands that each one of us behave in an honest and forthright manner. Therefore, *any kind of misrepresentation* is prohibited. It is of little importance whether the specific action is understood to be "theft" as the Ritva rules, or "falseness" as Rabbi Jonah Gerondi suggests. What is certain beyond any doubt is that the directive against *genevat da'at* is founded in Torah law.

What's more, it is foolish for anyone to think that any misdeed is ever without witness. A misdeed is *always* witnessed. Perhaps not by a fellow but certainly by God. And most certainly by one's own heart.

## WHAT IS GENEVAT DA'AT?

It is forbidden to sell meat which has not been ritually slaughtered in the proper way if the buyer understands that he is purchasing meat which had been correctly slaughtered.

One who sells another an object with a blemish must inform the buyer of the blemish even if the object is worth the price asked for with the blemish.

Casks of wine, which must be opened for sale, should not be broached in such a way as to deceive a guest and make him believe that they had been opened in his honor.

One should not invite his neighbor to eat at his table if he knows quite well that the invitation will be refused.

One should not pretend to give another a present knowing full well that the other will not accept it.

One should not say one thing with the mouth and mean something different in the heart; nor show one's neighbor one intends to honor him but not really mean it deep in the heart.

These examples appear in the Talmud, the *Mishnah Torah*, and the *Shulchan Aruch*. They are quite specific, and very telling. I'm sure it is not much of a stretch for any of us to imagine ourselves in a situation very similar to those that are expressly forbidden here. How many times have we praised – or acquiesced in praise of – a co-worker who we felt was undeserving of such praise? How many of us have "re-gifted" something, passed along a present that we did not really care for or want? How many of us have sold – or given away – a car knowing that there was a – very minor! – "blemish" having to do with its transmission or engine, or perhaps some hidden rusting of the chassis?

How many of us have phoned someone *when we knew they wouldn't be available* specifically to be able to leave a message on the machine rather than speak to the person directly?

These everyday examples are almost dismissible in their triviality. Goodness, *everyone* does things like that, don't they? What's the big deal? None of these things is likely to really hurt anyone. What's the big deal? They are minor trespasses at their worst, right?

They certainly don't represent the kind of blatant lies that cause real damage. So, What's the harm?

There's that question again. What's the harm? What's the big deal? What are those rabbis getting so riled about?

Ironically, the rabbis understood these kinds of trespasses to be *exactly as trivial* as one might argue. However, to them, it is the triviality, the everydayness of the trespasses which makes them so dangerous. They are "soft" lies. "Gentle" lies. Even, "well meaning" lies. As such, they are generally hidden from the person that they are directed at. Isn't it better to "protect" another's feelings than tell the truth?

Perhaps one could try to argue that it is so but our rabbis would vehemently disagree. In fact, they believed that these trespasses are *worse* than blatant lies precisely because of their hidden nature. To them, the fact that "no one knows" is their greatest harm. They are more serious than outright theft *because of*, not despite, their insidious nature.

In Exodus 22:17 the Torah makes an unwavering judgment against, of all things, witches. "You shall not allow a witch to live."

Why would the Torah deem the behavior of curious and strange people who are engaged in activities that both the Rambam and the Ramban make

clear are neither idolatry nor a cult? What is so noxious about the behavior
of witches as to deem it worthy of death? Quite simply, witchcraft is dependent on deception. It targets the uneducated and deceives them. It ex-
ploits people by deception. The deception lies in the skillful presentation of
one thing as its not. Which is the very same flaw that rests at the heart of
*genevat da'at.*

No different than a shell game, it seeks to divert attention by means both
subtle and unsubtle and it does not matter what the aim is, the flaw is in the
*intent.*

The Rambam makes his feelings about the *halacha* of *genevat da'at* clear
when he wrote, "A person should always cherish truthful speech, an upright
spirit, and a pure heart free from all forwardness and perversity."

In these remarks, the Rambam is placing prohibitions against *genevat da'at*
in a position that is completely consistent with the entire thrust of Jewish law
and ethics. The "inside" must match the "outside" in Judaism. It is not enough
to "appear" holy if you are not similarly pure in your heart. Likewise, a person of true spirituality will always have that spirituality mirrored in his or her
outward appearance.

The Torah is clear. A Jew must present to the world a true reflection of his
inner self. To be a "nation of priests" demands nothing less. Deception has no
place in such a nation.

The Torah stands opposed to such childish formulas as, "sticks and stones
may break my bones but words will never hurt me." That is patently false.
Hurtful and wrong words hurt two people, the recipient and the speaker. The
Torah expressly forbids one to wrong another with words. The Talmud elaborates on this theme in a discussion of Leviticus 25:17. "You will then not be
cheating one another. You shall fear your God, since it is I Whom am God
your Lord."

Some readers might presume that this verse refers to cheating in matters
of business but our Sages point out that this cannot be the case because there
are many, many other verses that deal specifically with monetary matters.
Our Sages are clear in understanding this verse to refer to the "wronging with
words" – an offense which they held to be as serious, if not more so, than dishonesty in business.

Our Sages taught that, as wrong as it is to steal, that wrong is not necessarily irredeemable. It is possible to return or replace that which was stolen.
However, in the case of *ona'at devarim*, the wronging with words, the harm is
insidious and more permanent. Once spoken, words cannot be taken back.
They continue in a reality defined by themselves. In Shakespeare's words –
a poet, not a rabbi:

Who steals my purse steals trash: 'tis something, nothing;

Twas mine, 'tis his, and has been slave to thousands;

But he that filches from me my good name

Robs me of that which not enriches him.

And makes me poor indeed.

To wrong one with words is not limited to insults or even wrongful accu-
sations. The ways to wrong one with words are as varied and infinite as the
many ways it is possible to "damn with faint praise" or create a rhetorical
falsehood to flummox another. In fact, wronging with words can be as "in-
nocuous" as being playful with a shopkeeper. For example, bothering a shopkeeper with questions about how much his goods cost when you have no
intention of making a purchase.

Note that intention is essential here. There is nothing wrong with asking
about prices or comparative shopping. What is wrong is *posing* as a shopper
when you have no intention of buying.

Conversely, if you go into a shop looking for an item and the shopkeeper
does not carry it, he wrongs you with words if he directs you to someone
who cannot supply the item either, even if the intent is for the buyer to take
interest in some other item.

Are there any words spoken more fondly than, "Remember when?" These
words can be an invitation to fond reminisces and happy recollections of good
times. However, if these very same words are used to remind a man of his former bad ways after he has repented then they represent a terrible transgression. If someone has wronged you and has come to you with sincere
repentance and you have forgiven that person then it is wrong for you to remind that person of the wrong. Even if he has wronged you again.

There are few people in the Jewish community as revered as teachers. For
teachers carry the hope and promise of the future in their hands when they

set about the task of educating. However, has there ever been a teacher who has not stood in front of a classroom and looked upon a gathering of students, recognizing one who he knew had not prepared adequately *and asked that student for the answer to the question?* To ask a question of one whom you know does not know the answer is wronging that person with words.

The student is wrong to be ill-prepared but the teacher commits a graver trespass to wrong the student in such a way.

WHAT'S THE BIG DEAL?

In all of the above examples, we are confronted by what some might call a "victimless crime." In other words, what real harm is done by the examples I've given. Oh sure, the student might feel a reddening of the neck because he's embarrassed by his lack of preparation, but some would argue that he should bear the responsibility for that. In such scenarios, there really is no "victim" in any malicious sense. No property was stolen. No money lost.

Just like the student who cheats on an exam, we might find ourselves in these situations and ask, "What's the big deal? It's not as if I'm stealing something."

Of course, it should come as no surprise that such a self-serving and defensive retort would fall short in the face of the level of honesty and ethics Jewish law expects and demands. Rashi, quoting the Siphra, anticipates the reasoning when he offered his commentary on the verse, "You shall not vex your fellowman." In his very accessible manner, Rashi addresses the verse directly: "Here Scripture warns against vexing by words – that one should not annoy his fellow man, nor give him an advice which is unfitted for him, but is in accordance with the plan and the advantage of the adviser."

Sounds pretty straightforward. However, up until this point, Rashi has not addressed the fundamental questions, Who is Going to Know?

But lest you should say, "Who knows it whether I had any intention to do him evil?" Scripture therefore states, "but you shall fear your God"! He Who Knows men's thoughts, he knows it! In all cases where it is a matter of conscience, when no one knows the truth except the one who has the thought in his heart, Scripture always states: "But be afraid of your God.

There is no such thing as a "victimless crime." There is no such thing as a trespass without witness. There are always at least two witnesses – the one who trespasses and God. When you betray your fellow, you are betraying yourself and your good nature. You know it. And more importantly, God knows it.

There is the story of the man who enters a butcher shop and sees that the clerk is alone in the shop. The master is no where to be seen.

"Where is your master?"

"He has gone for the afternoon," the clerk replied.

At which point, the customer glanced over his shoulder and then approached the counter. "Well then, with your master out, you must give me a good measure then," he said with a wink, suggesting that the cut of meat and the weight should be more favorable than usual.

The clerk narrowed his eyes at the customer. "My master is always in," he replied.

Which is exactly the Torah's message. The Master is *always* in. Our Master is always watching and He expects of us, "a pure heart free from all forwardness and perversity."

## IT COULD BE WORSE...

There are those who might suggest that, even while acknowledging that God is watching, there is still a significant difference between the kinds of "wrongful behavior" outlined above and something "really wrong" like robbery. They might, perhaps, make a good case in a court of law but in the court of Jewish morality, their argument falls flat. In Judaism, there is no *moral* distinction between a "small" or a "large" sin. Of course, as in the case of civil law, Judaism metes out greater punishment for the greater "civil" crime. The world, after all, must balance between the theft of a million dollars versus the theft of a pocketful of change. (Even so, there is no objective measure here. The theft of a million dollars from a very, very wealthy man might be less of an offense than the theft of ten dollars from one for whom that represents an entire life savings.)

Unlike civil law, where the physical facts of a trespass are called into play (how much was taken, etc.) Judaism holds that the violation *itself* is the same in either instance. Many violations that are *she'in bo ma'aseh* – without specific physical action – are of greater offense than those which are *sheyesh bo ma'aseh* – in which there is a physical trespass. Even if the punishment is more harsh for the physical trespass!

In short, Judaism is not interested in excuses like, "but it was only *one* answer I cheated on" or, "I only plagiarized on a class assignment, not on something I was paid for." There is no trespass which is morally less or greater than the other. As in the case of it being impossible to be "just a little bit pregnant" it is equally impossible to be "a little bit" in violation of *genevat da'at*.

You are. Or you aren't.

In Judaism, actions in the world are mirrored reflections of the person you are on the inside and the person you are on the inside is a mirrored reflection of your actions in the world. *Genevat da'at* and *ona'at devarim* are both expressions of a flawed character and, as such, not subject to rationalizations. There is no justification for these trespasses because they do not result from rational responses to "realities" but rather are expressions of a fundamental inner flaw.

While excuses and rationalizations might find champions in a world that has no firm moral code, Judaism does not countenance them. Try as you might, you cannot "argue away" these trespasses. Attempting to do so brings to mind the fable of the turtle and the scorpion.

A scorpion, being a very poor swimmer, asked a turtle to carry him on his back across the river. "Are you mad?" exclaimed the turtle. "I know you. You will sting me while I am swimming and I will drown."

"My dear turtle," the scorpion chuckled, "where is the sense in that? If I were to sting you while you are swimming, it is true that you would drown but I would drown with you. Now where is the sense in that?"

"You are right," agreed the turtle. With that, he invited the scorpion to "hop on!" The scorpion climbed up on to the turtle's shell and then the turtle began to make his way across the river. Half-way across, the scorpion inflicted a mighty sting on the turtle. Paralyzed by the scorpion's poison, they both begin to sink to the bottom of the river. Before going under the water, the turtle looked at the scorpion and with a sad, resigned expression said, "You told me that there would be no sense in your stinging me, that we would both drown. And you were right. So then, why did you do it?"

"It has nothing to do with sense or logic," the scorpion sadly replied as the waters splashed up over the turtle's shell. "It is just my character."

Just like the scorpion, whose deeds have no sense or logic, the *gonev da'at* also functions without logic or sense. He too acts based on his nature and character. The only thing the behavior accomplishes is to blur the boundary between right and wrong, good and evil, truth and deception.

When values are compromised, moral confusion follows with unethical behavior right on its heels.

The "slippery slope" of offenses is made clear by the Torah. "You shall not steal, neither deal falsely, neither lie to one another." Rashi, quoting Siphra, explained the significance of this litany. "If you steal, you will in the end come to deny it, then you will lie (in order to back up your first denial), and ultimately, you will swear falsely."

Rather than rationalize this broken behavior, the offender should attempt to perform *t'shuvah*, to eradicate the flaws in character that allow such offenses to flourish. One should strive for the "upright spirit and pure heart" so valued by God.

## THE SEVERITY OF *GENEVAT DA'AT*

Many commentators look to the Eighth Commandment – Thou Shalt Not Steal – as speaking directly to the sin of *genevat da'at*. They make the argument that stealing inevitably leads to lying, and taking false oaths. In addition, it is clear that it causes emotional suffering. The Mechilta is more exact: "There are seven categories of thieves. "Foremost among them is the *gonev da'at he'beriyot*." More to the point, it is considered a greater offense to mislead or misrepresent than to steal, since "False, misleading lips is a grave sin and we have been forewarned regarding the essence of truth, which is the foundation of our existence."

There is no question that our Sages spoke with one voice in considering that misleading someone is a graver trespass than to out and out lie to them. The question is, Why? Why is this offense considered so damaging? Why would the transgressor of this trespass be placed at the head of the list of thieves? It is astonishing and at odds with a modern sensibility, in which mere things are deemed more precious than the soul.

In Judaism, the inner self and outer sense must act in concert. Both are essential to living the life God would want for us. The peculiar and particular nature of our inner beings make them vulnerable to deception. And therein lies the true danger – the inherent potential for *genevat da'at* to bring lasting harm to our souls.

To be guilty of *genevat da'at* is to be guilty of a trespass that cannot be undone. There is no question, to steal is a grave offense. However, the thing that has been stolen can be returned or compensated for. The physical world allows for physical correction. However, to mislead or to misrepresent can never be amended. The consequences can be more far-reaching.

Theft, for all the hurt it causes, has its roots in need or in greed – in physical motivations which can be pitied or decried. *Genevat da'at* can have no such motivations. He who transgresses does so only to harm – and in an insidious manner that can be difficult to recognize at first.

When an item is stolen, it is gone. We can measure the absence. When we are deceived that which has been taken is beyond dimension.

Rabbi Norman Amsel writes about these immeasurable implications in his essay, "Teaching Students to Cheat or Not to Cheat."

[There was a] bright, creative, and personable young man who was very popular in school. Throughout high school he cheated on almost every test by devising ingenious methods to avoid getting caught. Being popular, his friends never told on him. He then cheated on the SAT exam and got into a good college, where he continued to cleverly cheat and get good grades. When he cheated on his Medical Boards, he was admitted into medical school where he also cheated and graduated without learning very much. Because of his good personality, he built up a private practice and he is now a doctor... He very well may be your doctor (without you knowing it) and may hurt many people. The same story could be told of a lawyer, accountant, rocket scientist, or any other professional.

## KIDDUSH HASHEM AND *GENEVAT DA'AT*

There are two types of *genevat da'at*, each associated with a different Biblical verse. The first is the "cases" type where, as in the example above, the serious consequences of deceit are obvious. The Smag, a Biblical commentator, cites a verse from Samuel as the basis for prohibiting this type of misrepresentation. "And Absalom stole the hearts of the men of Israel." In this instance, we see Absalom deceiving the people of Israel by leading them to falsely believe that King David would not resolve their disputes. His misleading and misrepresentation has clear and obvious implications. Such deception is the common understanding of *genevat da'at*.

Sadly, and dangerously, there are many other instances when the implications and consequences of deception are not so clearly recognized – and therefore, not so readily addressed. The Smag cites the story of Jacob as an example of this deeper, and more destructive, form of *genevat da'at*.

Although our Sages hold Jacob to be the very embodiment of *emet* – truth – one episode sharply counters this understanding. When Jacob ran away from his father-in-law, Lavan, without informing him, he was being deceitful. According to the Torah, Jacob "stole the heart of Lavan."

One might argue, What was Jacob to do? Had he told Lavan of his intention to leave, Lavan would surely have forbidden his departure. What's more, Jacob's purpose in leaving was to fulfill God's command to return to the Land of Israel. Certainly such an intent overrides Lavan's needs, particularly when we remember that Lavan had himself dealt dishonestly with Jacob!

Despite these formidable arguments, the Torah is clear. Jacob *stole* Lavan's heart. In the Hebrew, *vayignav*. Both the *Targum Yonatan* and Ibn Ezra affirm that Jacob's act was indeed an act of *genevat da'at*.

When Lavan catches up with Jacob, he cries to him, "What have you done, that you stole away my heart, and led away my daughters as captives taken away with the sword? Wherefore did you flee away secretly, and steal away from me?"

Can we justify such an act of *genevat da'at* from the very model of *emet*?

Jacob's behavior was more deceptive than Absalom's. In Jacob's case, it is necessary to probe deeper to recognize the implication of his dishonesty. He

does not, as Absalom did, make a clearly untrue statement. Rather, by his behavior *he has avoided the opportunity to sanctify God's name.* In every public display
of the truth, God's name is sanctified.

Jacob's actions do not appear harmful at first glance. Indeed, they are easily rationalized by those who look first to the glory of man rather than the
glory of God. But the truth remains – he *should* have acted righteously as a
means of *Kiddush Hashem* – sanctifying God's name.

The Rambam weighs the great merit of *Kiddush Hashem* against the
equally great offense of *Hillul Hashem* – the desecration of God's name.
There are other things that are a profanation of the Name of God.
When a man, great in the knowledge of Torah and reputed for his piety
does things which cause people to talk about him, even if the acts are
not express violations, he profanes the Name of God... The greater a
man... the more scrupulous should he be in all such things, and do
more than the strict letter of the law requires.

According to the Rambam, *genevat da'at* then is not solely the performance
of a deceptive act but that *by definition* the absence of a positive act (*Kiddush
Hashem*) represents an offense, and therefore *genevat da'at.*

Clearly, the demand of such holy performance is greater for those who
are more pious. The greater the piety, the greater the expectation. Jacob,
the embodiment of *emet*, was obligated to act positively to perform *Kiddush Hashem.* Failure to do so was an act of *Hillul Hashem.* While his intention was lofty and his goal divine, he "was staying with ignorant
people and living among them." Therefore his behavior must be judged
more harshly.

In order to truly sanctify God's name, a Jew must be,
scrupulous in his conduct, gentle in his conversation, pleasant toward
his fellow creatures, affable in manner when receiving them, not re-
torting, even when affronted, but showing courtesy to all, even to those
who treat him with disdain, conducting his commercial affairs with integrity... such a man has sanctified God.

*Kiddush Hashem* demands a positive posture. It requires action. Avoiding
desecration is not sufficient to sanctify God. Sanctification is not the absence

of desecration. It is the positive embrace of that which is holy and right. Mere avoidance of *genevat da'at* is not enough. Jacob's name is diminished by this episode because he missed the opportunity to openly and honestly communicate with Lavan. As a result, the *Kedushat Levi* notes that Jacob was detained unnecessarily by Lavan. Had he openly displayed righteous behavior during the many years of his sojourn with his father-in-law he would have been able to leave freely, with no need of deception.

The Chatam Sofer expresses amazement at Jacob's missed opportunity.
It is surprising that Jacob fled. For after God told him to go leave this land, he should have trusted in God, and should have left openly and not as one who flees after committing a theft or trickery. It may have been because of this that Dina his daughter was stolen from him in a similar fashion.

Could Jacob – or anyone else – have foreseen such a consequence to his deceptive action? For this reason, the Smag offered two verses as examples of *genevat da'at*.

## Kiddush Hashem and Hillul Hashem

The dynamics of *Kiddush Hashem* and *Hillul Hashem* add a vital dimension to our discussion of *genevat da'at*. More important than our parsing the significance of falsely obtained grades and diplomas, more important than acts of dishonesty in commerce, there is the issue of whether God's name will be sanctified or desecrated by our behavior and actions.

Falsely obtaining a grade or diploma is an offense precisely because, at its base, it is a desecration of God's name.

Rabbi Moshe Feinstein, *zt"l* gave this responsum regarding the stealing of Regents examinations and *genevat da'at*:
Concerning your question as to what you heard that in Yeshivot they permit their students to steal the Regent Examinations in order to pass their courses, it is prohibited not only because of the principle that the law of the land is binding but also by Torah law. It is not only deception which is prohibited in accordance with Shmuel who said (*Hullin* 94) that it is prohibited to deceive people which includes even non-Jews, and how much more so in these cases where it involves deceiving the

population at large which includes Jews, but it is also pure theft. This is because in the future when the person who cheated will pursue a career his potential employer will, for the majority of the time desire a person who satisfactorily completed his secular education and will hire him based upon his degree (which was earned dishonestly). Since his hiring is based upon a deception, the salary which he will receive will be considered stolen.

And do not err and justify such actions, by saying that the employer is concerning himself with irrelevant information and therefore a person can lie about such issues, for the following reasons. Firstly, even if generally employers aren't concerned, this employer has demonstrated his concern. Secondly, it is always prohibited to lie even if nothing bad will result for it is not one of the three things mentioned in the Talmud (*B.M.* 23) when it is permissible to alter the truth. Additionally, if the employer knew he was lying he would not trust him at all. Likewise, since this person learned in a yeshiva (thus giving him a reputation of integrity, honesty, and responsibility), the employer will blame people for mishaps when there were in fact his responsibility, and would fire the other person for he would never suspect a *talmid chacham*. But if he knew that he cheated in school he wouldn't be so quick to suspect and fire the other person.

Additionally, here in our country employers are particular that their workers have a good education, for people who are secularly trained know more about business. Therefore, it is prohibited to cheat even if as a result he will be able to learn Torah, for even for the sake of learning Torah it is prohibited to steal.

It is clear why our Sages and authorities include *genevat da'at* as a form of theft, forbidden by the eighth commandment. The misrepresentation is an offense in and of itself. It invariably leads to further transgressions and countless other consequences. The *Hillul Hashem* which inevitably results from such deception is beyond redemption.

**Al Chet**

During Yom Kippur, when we have our final opportunity to ask forgiveness for our many trespasses before the Book of Life is closed on another year, we recite the prayer, *Al Chet*, in which we enumerate the many different kinds of transgressions that we have committed over the course of the year. It is a public confession of our actions for which we, as a community, ask for God's forgiveness.

The character of this prayer is that it is spoken in the plural. This is not to suggest that our transgressions are somehow "shared" but rather that our sins affect not just our individual selves but our communal self as well. In this way, we can understand how our personal behavior impacts the community.

Our rabbis and teachers have often spoken of the power and significance of this prayer in calling our attention to the themes of the High Holidays. However, often overlooked in these teachings has often been the emphasis that this prayer places on ethical behavior. A close examination of the *Al Chet* prayer would show that fully sixteen of its verses deal directly with issues of honesty and integrity in monetary matters, the ethics of the marketplace.

This prayer, composed long before there existed the "modern marketplace" nonetheless speaks eloquently about the need to behave honestly and ethically in our dealings.

### By Acting Callously

The *Al Chet* calls our attention to our callousness. It is true that we often "turn our backs" and act callously to our fellows but this is a moral issue. What could this have to do with business ethics? Every Jew is expected to give ten percent of his earnings for charitable purposes. The withholding of this charity is callous and therefore unethical. Certainly if we were to criticize or humiliate a staff person – particularly in front of others – we are acting callously. Honest and ethical behavior demands that we treat our peers, business partners, staff and customers with respect, regardless whether they are Jews or non-Jews.

### Both in Public and in Secret

Public deception is generally frowned upon even in the business world. Why? Because there is a greater likelihood of getting caught! But, with the

Master always in, "getting caught" is not the standard. Behaving ethically is. Therefore, both public and secret deception is contrary to Jewish law and ethics. Insider trading. Failure to make full disclosure. Selling defective merchandise, using false weights or deceptive packaging... these are all examples of secret deception that is forbidden.

Certainly, copying of tapes, computer programs, and the downloading of copyrighted music would all fall under secret deception as well!

### Knowingly and Deceitfully

Jewish law is quite specific – it is forbidden to deceive or mislead people in any and all matters of the marketplace. Jew or Gentile, this law is clear. No deceit!

### Oppressing a Fellow

Having experienced slavery, it is anathema to Jews to oppress another. However, there are many "soft" forms of oppression which must be avoided. By overcharging for our goods and services, or taking excessive profits, we are guilty of oppressing our customers. The Jewish world view is not a strictly "capitalist" view. We do not hold to the standard of "whatever the market will bear." Rather, we cannot take unfair advantage of conditions or customers for our monetary gain. For example, during severe weather conditions, it would be unthinkable in Jewish law that a Jewish shopkeeper would increase the price of certain goods and items to take advantage of an emergency or disaster.

### By Violence

Violence is brought to bear in many ways, not just by the use of physical force. Sometimes we do violence to another by withholding *their* ability to exercise their legitimate options and strengths. We do this in many ways. For example, if we withhold wages or misuse funds that have been entrusted to us, we are denying people the benefit of what belongs to them.

### By Defaming God's Name

Clearly, anything that does not bring honor to God's name detracts from it. We have established this dynamic clearly. If we are not actively performing *Kiddush Hashem* we are engaged in *Hillul Hashem*. The Talmud clearly indicates that economic deception is one of the most clear cut and common examples of *Hillul Hashem*.

### Wittingly and Unwittingly

It is human to rationalize, to allow ourselves to "sink" to the common level. When we accept prevailing standards in the business world, we inevitably are accepting standards far below those required by Jewish law. Jewish law and tradition demand a higher level of honesty, not just the minimization of deceit.

### By Fraud and Falsehood

While it would be a foolish shopkeeper who would purposefully have an unattractive window display in his shop, it is wrong to present goods and services in a way that takes advantage of a customer's ignorance or naiveté. Deceptive advertising, extravagant claims, or concealing defects or faults in products are all forbidden by Jewish law.

### Ensnaring people

There is, perhaps, no more difficult sales position for an ethical Jew than to be a car salesman. The caricature of a car salesman is one who would sell someone any car on the lot. And yet, it is forbidden in Jewish law to mislead naïve clients. Better to sell a good car at a fair price.

### By Breach of Trust

This, of course, goes to the very heart of our relations with others – whether social or in business. Every relationship depends on trust. Even contractual agreements depend on trust in the fairness of the contract and the rule of law. A "handshake" agreement or verbal agreement is even more dependent on trust.

Trust is meaningless without honesty. Any words or actions that compromise honesty, compromise trust and, ultimately, the fabric of all our social and business relationships.

### THE COMPLEXITIES OF TRUTH AND LYING

Our inherent ability to lie troubled the angels when God was about to create man. The Midrash relates how, "The ministering angels divided into two parties. Mercy said, 'Create him.' Truth said, 'Do not create him, since he is all falsehood.'"

The rejection of dishonesty and the embrace of truth is our central challenge as human beings. All other ennobling goals depend on how we answer that challenge. However, the task of attaining truth is not always a straightforward enterprise. It is told of the Hasidic leader, the *Ba'al HaTanya*, that he strove for twenty-one years to truly grasp and accomplish truthfulness. For seven years, he struggled to determine what truth is. For seven more, he wrestled with *sheker*, falsehood. Finally, he spent seven more years fully integrating truth into his personality.

Would that the process were so linear !

There is the story of a mate on a sailing vessel...

One night, the mate becomes drunk for the first time in his life. When he sees that the captain has written "Mate drunk today" in the ship's log, the mate implores him to erase it, as it will reflect badly on him. "After all," he argues, "it is my first offense." The captain refuses, saying, "This is the truth, and into the log it goes."

Some days later, the mate makes his own entry into the log. "Captain sober today." When the captain sees it, he protests, claiming that it makes it appear as though his sobriety is a rare occurrence. But the mate echoes the captain's own words, "This is the truth, and into the log it goes."

When are we instructed to tell the truth? Is there such a thing as a "half-truth"? A "half-lie"? What of Rashi's "white lies" which are permitted for the sake of *shalom habayit*?

What does the Torah demand of us who live in this real world?

There are two Torah sources that prohibit lying. Leviticus states, "Do not lie to one another." Exodus, which not only prohibits lying but also instructs, "From a false matter you shall distance yourself." Sforno states that the verse from Exodus makes clear that one must refrain from saying anything that may be construed to be a lie.

It would seem clear why the Torah would command us not to deal falsely with one another. After all, if people deal falsely with one another, the very fabric of community is torn apart. However, the need to distance ourselves from falsehood is not quite so self-evident. Yet our tradition is just as clear about the one as the other. The Talmud speaks to the verse in Exodus, "Keep far from ugly dealings and that which savor of them, or even remotely resembles them."

In this we once again see the that in Judaism a double negative does not make a positive. "Not lying" is not "telling the truth." Likewise, falsehood is more than simply not telling the truth. Falsehood is everything and anything which runs counter to wisdom and the accepted codes of appropriate conduct.

It is appropriate and right to treat your fellow fairly. Failure to do so is therefore falsehood. It follows from this that ingratitude, misrepresentation, and disrespect must therefore also be forms of falsehood.

The command to distance ourselves from falsehood is more than a command to avoid that which is wrong. It is a command to *do* what is right.

Distancing ourselves from falsehoods removes the semblance of misrepresentation from our words and deeds. In this way, we avoid even the intimation that a falsehood has occurred.

By this criteria, the actions of the ship's mate would be forbidden, for they invite misunderstanding and misrepresentation.

Judaism is firm in demanding more than simply "not lying." It demands complete honesty and truth. Half-truths and false flattery are, as the Rambam explains, forbidden:

It is forbidden to accustom oneself to smooth speech flatteries. One must not say one thing and mean another. Inward and outward self should correspond; only what we have in mind should we utter with the mouth. We must deceive no one, not even an idolater… Even a single word of flattery or deception is forbidden. A person should always cherish truthful speech, and a pure heart free from all forwardness and perversity.

This would seem to be the "last word" on this topic. And yet... and yet it can't be. Our lives are too complex and the issue too often existing in gray rather than black and white. Certainly there must be *some* instances when waiving the truth is permitted in the interest of greater values and goals. Of course, there is. The Torah provides such an example.

When Abraham and Sarah were visited by the strangers, God Himself amended Sarah's words for the sake of *shalom habayit* – domestic tranquility and peace. In this episode, in which the strangers foretell of Sarah giving birth to Abraham's child, despite their advanced ages, Sarah laughed within herself and said, "After I am grown old shall I have pleasure, and my lord being old also?" However, when God relates this to Abraham, He said, "Wherefore did Sarah laugh, saying 'Will I surely give birth when I am old?'"

The discrepancy between what Sarah actually says and what God relates to Abraham is clear. However, our Sages view this type of emendation of the truth as permissible because it promotes peace and is not intended in any way to benefit the one party or diminish the other.

In short, if promoting genuine peace requires the withholding the truth, then it is not necessarily a falsehood. In fact, such an attempt at peace making might even be considered a *mitzvah*. The Talmud teaches that, "it is permissible to deviate in the interest of peace... R. Nathan said, 'it is a religious thing to do.'" We similarly recall Joseph's brothers telling him after his father's death, "Your father did command before he died, saying, 'so shall you say to Joseph: forgive, I ask you, the transgression of your brothers.'"

However, even in this instance, the ability to differentiate is not always clear. A husband who has wronged his wife cannot lie about his wrong simply because he knows his wife will be angry. He has already destroyed the underlying foundation of peace. He cannot then use that as an excuse to avoid the consequences of his actions.

The Talmud addresses the issue of flattery and "white lies" in the tractate *Ketubot*. Beit Shammai and Beit Hillel, are in customary debate, this time over the custom of always complimenting the beauty of a bride. When a bride is indeed beautiful, one is merely speaking the truth to say so. However, what happens when the bride is not attractive?

Beit Shammai states that such a compliment would then be a lie, and is therefore forbidden. Beit Hillel, however, takes the opposing view, saying it is permissible to call her beautiful even when it is obviously not the case. Rav Moshe Taragin elaborates:

Beit Shammai (one might say characteristically) adopts the "hard-line" position that the truth must be pursued at all costs, even if that compromises the feelings of the *kalla* [bride]. They maintain that one may only pronounce "ka*lla kemot she-hi* [the bride is as she is] – effectively, he must tell it as it is. Conversely, Beit Hillel maintains that [it] is permitted to praise the *kalla* as *"na'a ve-chasuda"*, comely and pleasing, even though his flattery is mendacious.

The Ritva notes that the basis for Hillel's position is *darchei shalom* – the paths of peace. "In order to avoid controversy and bruised emotions, the [it] is permitted to alter the truth and offer his compliments." However, it is once again important to make clear that the exemptions to truthfulness are few and far between and that the justifications are very specific. The justifications for such an exemption *never* include the rationalization of one's own deceptions and lies.

Indeed, so intertwined are deception and flattery that the most pious go to great lengths to avoid flattery. As in this example concerning the Brisker Rov:

Back in the founding days of the State of Israel, the government sought to conscript all eligible young people into the Army – men and women. While there were many, many conflicts between the State and religious authorities in those early days, none was considered more serious than this particular issue. From the perspective of Jewish law, the government was seeking to undermine the most vital and basic foundation of Judaism in a wicked way. The conscription of women into the Israeli army was seen as a threat to the Jewish home for generations to come.

The religious authorities sought to oppose this edict with every fiber of their being. Rabbi Shlomo Lorincz suggested to the Chazon Ish that he write directly to Prime Minister Ben Gurion to express his strong feelings on the matter.

The Chazon Ish agreed to draft such a letter. There followed a discussion about who else should sign the letter. Rabbi Lorincz felt it very important that the Brisker Rov sign the letter for it to have its greatest impact.

The Chazon Ish shook his head. He had agreed to the letter but on the matter of the Brisker Rov's signature he held up his hand to dissuade the rabbi. "The Brisker Rov will not agree to such a thing," he announced.

"Why not?" the rabbi asked.

The Chazon Ish shrugged his shoulders. "It is not possible to apply to the Prime Minister with a request like this without some flattery." He paused. "The letter itself is a kind of flattery," he said. "The Brisker Rov, who is entirely *emes*, will never sign it."

As it happened, the Chazon Ish's words were shared with the Brisker Rov and he nodded his head to indicate that the Chazon Ish was correct, he would never sign such a letter. And so, the letter was sent to the Prime Minister with only the Chazon Ish's signature on it.

Years later, after the Chazon Ish's death, some religious authorities examined the actual letter that was sent and determined that there was not the slightest trace of flattery in it at all. However, the Chazon Ish felt that simply *writing the letter* indicated a level of flattery that would be unacceptable to the Brisker Rov.

It is important to remember that the issue that the letter addressed could not have weighed more heavily on the Brisker Rov. It was said that it disturbed his peace of mind to the very depths of his sensitive soul. He worked night and day to abolish the edict. His efforts affected his health. However, in the end, his efforts were, by the Grace of God, successful.

This incident speaks powerfully to how strongly the Brisker Rov associated flattery with deception. Even this issue, which so tormented his soul, was not sufficient reason for him to exercise even a shade of what he considered flattery. He would not deviate from the truth.

### THE IRREVOCABLE BOND OF TRUTH AND FAITH

Acknowledging those very rare and specific circumstances when a "white lie" is permissible, the command is clear: it is forbidden to cheat, deceive or to be false. The Torah even goes a step further. It is not enough to simply not engage in such behavior. We must actually distance ourselves from all dishonesty and falsehood. The message is clear. No one can stand close to the flame and avoid getting burned.

Our faith is dependent on our embrace of truthfulness. For our faith is the essence of the Torah and the commandments. "It entails," states Rabbeinu Bachya, "the belief that the universe has a Creator Whose existence is absolute; Who is One, and Whose providential care extends over this lower world, guarding the human species generally and specifically."

He continues that,

faith entails the obligation to love the truth, to prefer it, and to speak it, as the prophet Zechariah said, "These are the things that you shall do: Speak ye every man the truth with his neighbor; execute the judgment of truth and peace in your gates." This means that man must be pure in his speech and speak only the truth even in such matters that affect no one. He who unflatteringly adheres to the truth will merit having his prayers heard, as David said, "The Eternal is nigh until all that call upon Him, to all that call upon Him in truth." Furthermore, always acting in compliance with the truth brings one closer to God, Who is the true One, and grants one the prodigious reward and privilege of "life in the world to come."

Faith and truth are inherently connected, bound in the same intrinsic way that one's inner and outer selves are connected. One cannot exist without the other; one mirrors the other, reflecting it just as the one depends upon the other. In order to attain the ultimate reward, one must adopt and imitate God's attributes and walk in His ways. In commenting on the verse, "and you shall walk in His ways," the Sages elaborate:

Just as He is the merciful One, so should you be merciful. Just as He is the gracious One, so should you be gracious. Just as He clothes the naked, so should you clothe the naked. Just as He visits the sick, so should you visit the sick. Just as He comforts mourners, so should you comfort mourners. Just as He buries the dead, so should you bury the dead.

Just as God is holy, so should we strive for holiness. By doing so, we meld our way to the way of God, fulfilling the directive, "You should be wholehearted with the Eternal your God." To be "wholehearted" means to have an inner personality in harmony with one's external appearance and actions, to have "the principles of faith firmly planted in his heart and deeply engraved in his mind."

We see in all aspects of Jewish life and tradition the constant dialogue between the inner self and the outer self, the spiritual and the physical. Modern psychologists point to the conflict between the emotional (inner self) and the way a person behaves in the world (the outer self) as being the source of dissonance, of anxiety and depression. This does not come as a surprise to the Jewish community where we have always known that the inner self and outer self must be in congruence in order to live a life worthy of meaning and faith. How we behave must reflect who we are. It is in this way that we know that honesty and truthfulness are the ultimate expressions of Godliness.

O Eternal who shall sojourn in Your Tabernacle? Who shall dwell upon Your holy mountain? He that walks in wholeheartedness, and works righteousness.

The Torah, God's perfect revelation, is called Truth. As it says in Proverbs: Acquire the truth and sell it not," and "My mouth shall utter truth." All things in God's creation have meaning and significance. So it is that not just the meaning of words but the words themselves carry meaning. For example, the Hebrew word for truth, *emet*, is composed of three letters. Aleph. Mem. Tav. These three letters represent the first (aleph), the middle (mem), and the last (tav) letters of the Hebrew alphabet. What does this teach us? It teaches us that the Torah (as truth) is an all-inclusive source of truth, for the letters are the very building blocks, the foundation, of Torah.

The Talmud, the great compendium of Jewish learning, declares, "Truth is the seal of the Holy One, blessed be He, as it is said [in Jeremiah] "and the Eternal God is the true God." For this reason, we add the word *emet* at the end of the *Shema*, proclaiming the validity and truth of the words of faith we have just recited.

By loving the truth and dealing faithfully with others, we imitate and come closer to God and His Torah. We know that Truth is one of God's thirteen attributes, and it is His model of absolute truth and morality that we must strive to emulate. Human truthfulness entails being faithful to God *and to man*.

One without the other is a contradiction. To be honest in our dealings with God demands honesty in our dealings with our fellows and to be honest in our dealings with our fellows, by definition, means that we are performing *Kiddush Hashem*.

To speak truth even in one's heart is to be faithful to God and man. Refraining from cheating, plagiarizing, or engaging in any form of misrepresentation – in other words, distancing ourselves from all forms of deceit and hypocrisy – these are the first steps toward *emet*. Being honest and trustworthy – taking these positive steps and actions – represent faithfulness to God and man.

God is truth. He has given us the Torah as a guide to living truly and truthfully. The struggle towards honesty and the challenge of overcoming our human tendency for deception is what defines our struggle in this world. We must remember that even the smallest lie, the seemingly harmless falsehood enacted in the secrets places of our heart, is still forbidden.

After all, the Master is *always* in.

Nothing is hidden.

# THE DREIDLE

## THE MIRACLES IN OUR LIVES

*O Chanukah, O Chanukah come light the menorah;*
*Let's have a party, we'll all dance the* horah…

In my home, in the room where I keep my many books, I also keep an ever-growing collection of dreidles. These dreidles are in a variety of sizes and colors; they are made in a broad array of materials and they come from countries throughout the world – from here in the United States, from Israel, Spain, Hungary, India, Russia, Scotland.

My collection began with a kind of childlike delight I took in the dreidles. Few Jewish objects so quickly conjure up the joys of childhood as a dreidle! Who can hold a dreidle in his hands and not have a vivid memory of a crisp, chilly wintry evening? The sun is setting; there is the aroma of oil, with the satisfying smell of onions and potatoes frying.

Chocolate gelt is piled in front of cousins and friends. Each of you holds a dreidle. The game is about to begin…

However, no matter how evocative, memories are memories and it remained a curiosity that a man of my years would not only *have* such a collection but that he would continue to enthusiastically add to it.

When I considered the joy I took in my collection, I realized that it was not simply childhood memories that made my dreidle collection so important to me.

The essential message of Chanukah – and it is impossible to think of drei-dles without thinking of Chanukah – is the power of miracles. Aha! This then is the nexus of my deep, abiding and joyful relationship with dreidles. I have always believed in miracles – both the grand, historical miracles of Jewish history and the smaller, day-to-day miracles which make life so joyous and meaningful – none of which is more powerful to me personally than having met my wife on the second night of Chanukah six years ago!

Still, it seems more than curious that this little top could evoke such strong feelings. What is it about this little (or not so little) top that moves us and in-spires us?

The dreidels we see today are certainly different from the modest clay or wood dreidles of long ago. Consistent with the world in which we live, many "modern" dreidles are "hi-tech" and multi-media. They glow in strange ma-terials and flash with colored lights. The "dreidle song" no longer has to be sung because the music itself is played when some tops spin!

Just as Judaism brings together opposites in so many ways, embracing these very modern expressions of the *form* of the dreidle does not mean for-saking the fundamental meaning and lessons of the dreidle. If you were to transport a child from the 21st century, he or she would still recognize the dreidles used then, just as a child from the 15th century would still find joy and comfort in a modern dreidle. Why? Because every dreidle is defined by its ability to spin, its stem and the Hebrew letters: *Nun, Gimmel, Hay, Shin.*

In Judaism, form must serve meaning. So, what is the significance of these letters and why (with only one possible modification, which I will discuss below!) do they appear on every dreidle?

While there are more answers to this question than you may imagine, I think the most important is that these four letters, read correctly, teach us the history of the world and its ultimate purpose.

Which probably seems like a large task for such a modest little top!

To understand the answer, we need to understand something about what it means to be a person. According to Rabbi Lowe of Prague, every person is made up of three elements: the body, the soul and the mind. In Hebrew, *guf, nefesh,* and *sechel.*

To be a complete person who finds meaning in life, all three of these ele-ments must be God-directed.

Now, in the history of the world, various empires have tried to destroy the Jewish people. Each has tried to do so in different ways and by attacking one or more of these elements.

The Babylonian Empire attacked the Jewish body – *guf* - murdering and massacring us as they destroyed the First Temple in 586 b.c.e. and stole the Jewish people into captivity and exile in Babylon. The promiscuity of the Persian Empire – we learn in the story of Purim about Ahasverosh's harem – was a direct threat to the soul – *nefesh* – of the Jewish People. And the Greek Empire, defined by its learning and philosophy, threatened the *sechel* of the Jewish people by trying to falsely show that the Torah is incompatible with science.

However, none of these threats was as great as the one presented by the Roman Empire, which honed all three in a single, powerful threat (*hakol*), attacking the Jewish soul, body, and mind.

Ask any Jewish child what the Hebrew letters on the dreidle stand for and he or she is sure to say, "*Nes gadol haya sham!*" – a great miracle happened there. But, alas, we are not children and so we look beyond this straightforward explanation to an ever-deeper one. Therefore:

The *gimmel* on the dreidle represents the *guf* (Babylon); the *nun* represents the *nefesh* (Persia); the *shin* represents *sechel* (Greece); and the *hay* represents *hakol* (Rome).

What's more, every Hebrew letter has a numerical value. By using this numerical value, *gematria*, we can delve even deeper into the mystical meanings beyond the words. It happens that the *gematria* of *gimmel, nun, shin,* and *hay* is 358. Which is the very same *gematria* as *nachash* – the Hebrew word for the serpent that seduced Adam and Eve at the beginning of time.

Such an association would be interesting in and of itself but it is incomplete in a Jewish sense if we do not also recognize that it is also the same *gematria* as *mashiach* – the Messiah, the Redeemer of the Jewish People at the end of time!

All this in a little top! The history of the world from Eden until the end of time. The presence of evil (the serpent) has tormented the Jewish people throughout history but, in the end the serpent will be defeated by *mashiach*!

So many lessons in such a modest object!

The dreidle teaches us about God. Just as the dreidle spins around a central point and topples when it begins to lose its connection to that point, so too do we begin to "lose our footing" when we begin to lose our connection to our center.

The dreidle teaches us about our own psychologies. We are only "whole" when all the aspects of our being – body, mind, soul… hakol – are balanced and blended. When the dreidle spins, who can distinguish between each of the individual sides? No one! As we spin in perfect balance, on our central point, we are balanced and whole.

Perhaps most important, the dreidle teaches us these powerful lessons by being *fun*! The dreidle connects us through the liturgical year. The Chanukah dreidle spins from above (the stem is on top), teaching us that assistance and salvation come from God. The Purim groegger spins from below, teaching us that there are times when our help must come from within.

Ultimately, my fascination with dreidles comes from my fascination with miracles. We Jews are people of miracles. Not only do we believe in and appreciate miracles, our continued existence is truly miraculous.

Over three hundred years ago King Louis XIV of France asked Pascal, the great philosopher of his day, to give him proof of the existence of miracles. Without hesitation, Pascal answered, "Why, the Jews, your Majesty. The Jews."

At first glance, his answer would seem lacking at best. What must the king have made of it? We don't know that but we do know exactly what Pascal meant by his answer because he explained it all clearly in his masterwork, *Pensees.*

In *Pensees*, he made clear that the fact that the Jewish people had survived even to his day (he was ignorant, of course, of the threats to our existence yet to come!) was proof enough for him that there were miracles.

For no rational explanation existed to make sense of our continued presence upon the world's stage.

A more modern historian, Arnold Toynbee, wrote a ten-volume encyclopedia of human history. And in the course of those many volumes the one thing that seemed to trouble him was that only the continued flourishing of the Jewish people contradicted his "universal" rules that govern the inexorable decline of every peoples on earth.

Only the Jews.

Despite history's brutal attempts to destroy the children of Israel, we have managed to defy all predictions of our demise.

Just as we are able to look back at the famous, 1964 *Look* magazine cover that confidently predicted "The Vanishing American Jew" and smile (*Look* magazine no longer exists and yet, here we are!) we can look back over the sands of time and see the fall of the empires that sought our demise – from the Akkadians to the Babylonians to the Persians to the Third Reich.

Jewish history – indeed, Jewish *existence*, defies rational explanation.

The miraculous is so essential to who we are that David Ben Gurion, the first Prime Minister of the State of Israel, said, "A Jew who does not believe in miracles is not a realist."

The threats to our existence have come from without… and sometimes within. And *that* truth might teach us a great deal about the true Chanukah miracle – and add another chapter in the story of the dreidle.

\* \* \*

Chanukah was first celebrated more than two thousand years ago in Israel, then known as Judea. Because of the vagaries of the Jewish lunar calendar and the European solar calendar, the date when Chanukah is celebrated generally falls in late November or early December. However, the holiday itself never comes "early" or "late." It is always on the exact same date, year after year – the 25th day of the Hebrew month of Kislev.

The holiday celebrates our victory over King Antiochus Epiphanes, a pagan tyrant from Greece, who tried to destroy Judaism in 165 BC. It also celebrates the rededication of the Temple in Jerusalem.

To truly understand Chanukah, it is important to understand the history leading up to those difficult times and that means returning briefly back to the beginning of Jewish history.

During the time of Abraham, Isaac and Jacob, the Canaanites dominated the land God promised our forefathers, the land which would eventually become known as Judea, and then, Israel. After the conquest of the land under Joshua, when he led the Children of Israel back to the land after the Exodus, the land was parceled out to the twelve tribes according to the number of people in each tribe and the arability of the land. The tribe of Judah claimed the region from south of Jerusalem to the Negev desert. When David became king, he conquered Jerusalem, making it the capital of the united kingdom.

The kingdom split up after Solomon's death, and both Israel and Judah suffered continual deterioration for many generations. The Assyrians invaded Palestine in 721 B.C.E. and gained control of the north. In 606 B.C.E. and again in 586 B.C.E. the Babylonians under Nebuchadnezzar besieged Jerusalem and destroyed the First Temple, eventually bringing the whole land under their domination and taking many captives, including the prophet Daniel.

It was not until the Persians under Cyrus overthrew the Babylonians and freed the Jews from Captivity, allowing the Jews to return from Babylonia to their native land to rebuild the Temple and the walls of Jerusalem under Ezra and Nehemiah.

Cyrus' role was so profound in returning the Jews from Babylonian captivity that the prophet Isaiah refers to him as "God's anointed." "Thus says the Lord to his anointed (*l'mesheecho*), to Cyrus, whose right hand I have held, to subdue nations before him; and I will loose the loins of kings, to open before him doors and gates; and the gates shall not be closed." (Isaiah 45:1)

The Jews remained comfortably under Persian protection from about 500 B.C.E. to 330 B.C.E., at which time Persia was taken by Alexander the Great and Judea came under Greek domination.

All of this history is, well history, until the young Alexander the Great stepped onto the world stage. It is difficult for us to imagine the brilliance of the young Alexander. Not only was he a military genius but he seemed to take genuine interest in the countries which he conquered.

It is true that he introduced his Hellenic culture into the places he conquered, but he seemed also to find merit in the cultures of the places he conquered. By introducing Hellenic culture into Syria and Egypt, he had probably more influence on the development of Judaism than any other single non-Jew.

Some suspect that it is Alexander that Daniel refers to when he speaks of a mighty king who "shall stand up, that shall rule with great dominion." (Daniel 11:3) He is mentioned by name in the Apocryphal book of First Maccabees. Yet, the only historical event we have that connected Alexander with the Jews was recorded by Josephus and concerned his visit to Jerusalem after conquering Gaza. According to this account, Jaddua, the High Priest had received a warning from God in the form of a dream. In this dream he saw himself vested in a purple robe, with his miter – the one with the golden plate on which the name of God was engraved – on his head.

He went out to meet Alexander at Sapha followed by the priests, all clothed in fine linen, and by a multitude of citizens. When Alexander saw the high priest, he bowed and showed reverence for God and saluted the High Priest. In response, the Jews greeted Alexander with a single voice.

Alexander's general expressed dismay at this act. How could the one who deserved to be adored by all as king, adore the High Priest of the Jews? Alexander's response was simple and straightforward. "I did not adore him, but the God who has honored him with this high office." He went on to describe a dream in which he had foreseen the High Priest and from him had received instruction as to how he might conquer Asia.

Alexander than gave the High Priest his right hand and entered the Temple, where he offered sacrifice to God according to Jaddua's instructions.

The following day Alexander asked the people what favors he should grant them; and, at the high priest's request, he accorded them the right to live in full enjoyment of the laws of their forefathers. He, furthermore, exempted them from the payment of tribute in the seventh year of release. To the Jews of Babylonia and Media also he granted like privileges; and to the Jews who were willing to enlist in his army he promised the right to live in accordance with their ancestral laws.

While some historians doubt this account – a miraculous account in and of itself – Jewish legend seems to acknowledge the uniqueness of Alexander's influence on the Jews.

And it is here, that the seeds of the *real miracle* of Chanukah are planted. For the majority of Jews seemed only too happy to match Alexander's respect and honor for their religion with respect and honor for the Greek way of life. That is, Jewish culture became Hellenized – and *not by force* but by the willingness of the people to give up their heritage. The people were attracted to things Greek and were only too happy to turn away from the teachings of their fathers.

Under the gracious authority of Alexander, it seemed possible to have the "best of both worlds" – the rituals of the Temple, which Alexander respected, and the comforts of the Greek worldview.

Following the untimely death of Alexander only a handful of years later, there was thirty years of conflict as the lands of his conquest were divided amongst his generals.

After Alexander's death, Judea was ruled by the Greek families of the Ptolemies or the Seleucids, depending on which one was strongest in the area at the time. Despite the years of conflict, the Jews continued to live in relative peace. All that ended abruptly when the Seleucid king, Antiochus IV Epiphanes came to power. He insisted that the people engage in an ever greater degree of Greek culture, including the worship of the gods of the Greek pantheon. Even so, what remained most disconcerting was the sense that the people were almost complicit in the imposition of Greek culture in their lives. They seemed not to balk at each of these increasing demands.

Already acculturated to Greek life, each step on the slippery slope of assimilation was easier than the last. Perhaps if one would have asked the question, "Are you a Greek-Jew or a Jewish Greek?" (similar to the question sometimes posed in the United States – "are you an American-Jew or a Jewish American?"; a questions that seeks to measure the relative influence of being American or being Jewish in one's life) the majority would have claimed Greek-Jew. Perhaps they were proud of participating in Greek culture. Perhaps they loved the *gymnasia* more than they loved their own traditions.

Perhaps they thought of themselves as being more Greek than being Jewish. Or perhaps they really believed it no longer mattered. In other words, perhaps they had become assimilated in the dominant culture of their time and place.

All that is certain is that prior to the reign of Antiochus, the Jews lived in relative peace under various rulers and kings. Rulers came and went after Alexander but their lives were not much changed. Following Alexander's lead, each leader allowed the Jews to continue Temple worship and ritual.

At that time, the Temple in Jerusalem, the House of God, was the center of Jewish ritual life. It was the site of the three yearly pilgrimages the Jews took, bringing sacrifices to the priests. It contained all that was most holy to the people, including, in the Holy of Holies, the ark from the desert.

Before the Holy of Holies, the *ner tamid*, the eternal light, continually flickered, symbolizing our enduring and eternal faith.

All this changed with Antiochus. In short order, his wickedness and cruelty became more pronounced. He insisted that more and greater burdens be placed upon the Jews. They had to pay high taxes. He tried to force them to replace their Jewish laws and traditions with Greek ones. He even forced the Jews to accept a new high priest of his choosing, Menelaus.

The new high priest began to steal from the Temple and send precious gold and silver to Antiochus. Despite their embrace of many Greek ways, this insult angered the Jews and while Antiochus was fighting a war in Egypt, a small army of Jewish soldiers surrounded the temple to force Menelaus out.

Upon his return, Antiochus feared that the people were rising up against him so he ordered his army to storm the Temple.

The soldiers tore down the city walls and stripped the Temple of everything they could carry – all the gold and riches that Menelaus had not already stolen. The soldiers placed a Greek idol upon the golden altar and allowed pigs to run wild within the sacred grounds.

The people were threatened with death if they refused to worship the Greek idols. The soldiers laughed and mocked the Jews. They drank the holy water and set fire to books containing holy writings. Amongst all the chaos the soldiers sowed, the oil in the *ner tamid* was spilled and the inspirational light of the Temple dimmed.

Antiochus was wicked and cruel but he was also cunning. He'd sent his soldiers in to storm the Temple on the Sabbath so that the people would not fight back. Even for the Jews, lulled into a false sense of security by their assimilation, the Sabbath still called to them. In the carnage that followed, thousands of Jews were killed, maimed or carried off and sold as slaves.

We do not know how muffled the local protest was – if there was a protest at all – before the final insult of the storming of the Temple in Jerusalem by Antiochus' soldiers or the sacrifice to Zeus that was offered on the altar of burnt offering in the Temple that December of 168 B.C.E. Perhaps the people did not rise up to protest the edict that had been sent out to all the countryside that an altar to Greek gods was to be erected in every town in Palestine. For many, the appearance of officers to enforce the worship of Greek gods by every Jewish family was not overly troubling. After all, those officers were simply enforcing the reality that had already taken hold in the lives of the people.

Perhaps.

And perhaps not.

We do know that however muffled the protest in the rest of the country, it was not muffled everywhere in Modein. Whatever the mood throughout the rest of the country in regards to the edict to become "as the Greeks", it was not shared by everyone in that town. There, an old priest of the Lord, Mattathias, presided over the religious affairs of the community. When one of the Jewish people who had changed over to the Greek religion attempted to offer the first sacrifice to Zeus, Mattathias killed him.

This act committed, Mattathias then took off for the mountains with his five sons and their families.

With that, the real miracle began to unfold. *A people who had lost their sense of identity were about to rediscover themselves and their God.* This is the on-going miracle of the Jewish people. A country filled with Jews who had willingly compromised all that was best and dear about their identity as Jews had been called to the barricades. And they responded as to the voice of the ancient prophets. Jews flocked to the banner of Mattathias who, almost overnight, became the leader of rebellion against the Greeks under Antiochus IV.

In 166 B.C., Mattathias died, having appointed his third son, Judas (or, Judah), to lead the rebellion. (According to Josephus, Mattathias' great-great-grandfather was called Hasmon, so the family is known as the Hasmonean family.)

According to the second chapter of the first book of the Maccabees the surname of this now famous family was Maccabee, or Maccabaeus. The name is taken by many to mean "the hammer", from the Hebrew word *maqqabi*. And so Judas was called from the very outset, even before he began his military career, Judas, the Hammer.

Initially, the name "Maccabees" was applied Judas' family and kin but over time it was used to designate his close followers, and ultimately to all those who were champions of liberty and Jewish religion in the Greek period.

The military genius of Judas Maccabaeus was quickly evident. Over the next few years, he led the people in some of the most brilliant military successes in Israelite history. In quick succession the army of the Maccabees overthrew Syrian generals Appolonius, Seron, and Gorgias. After the regent Lysias, ruling for the Seleucid kings, had been defeated, he restored Temple worship in Jerusalem.

But genius is not a miracle. The glory of the Maccabbees in battle with the superior Greeks was not yet a miracle.

Even the oft-told story about the oil, in which a small jar found amidst the ruins of the Temple that was still sealed with a *heksher* attesting to its purity, a small jar with enough oil to maintain a light for a single day but which lasted a full eight days until other kosher oil could be found, is not the real miracle of Chanukah.

The two miracles of Chanukah – the victory of the Maccabees and the oil – do not represent the real miracle of Chanukah.

The real miracle of Chanukah, the one that is repeated so often in our history, is that a people who loses its way – lulled by the siren song of an appealing culture – and assimilates, losing the distinction of being God's chosen, once again finds itself.

* * *

The patriarch of the family pauses. The children look at him expectantly. He falls silent. In that silence, one of the children makes a face. "That doesn't sound like much of a miracle to me," she protests.

The grandfather smiles softly. "And what do you think sounds like a miracle?" he asks gently.

"That the oil lasted for eight days," she replies defiantly, crossing her arms to indicate that she feels quite strongly in the story as it had been told to her since she was a little child.

But her brother, the one who was soon to be called to the Torah as a Bar Mitzvah, recognizes something important in what his grandfather had taught. He was maturing and even some of the *midrashim* that he had loved so much as a young boy no longer animated his spirit. He understood that there were great forces in the world. History fascinated him. One of his teachers had asked the question, "How has this small people managed to survive the ages when the great civilizations of history – civilizations which have tried to crush her, have fallen?

He did not know the answer but he was convinced that something about the answer constituted a profound miracle.

"No," her brother says softly, gently disagreeing with his little sister. "I understand. The oil might be a miracle, but the greater miracle is what happens in the world and how it changes people, how it shapes our Jewish community."

The father, overhearing the discussion, feels his heart swell with pride. His son, already preparing his *maftir*, is indeed becoming a man.

"How do you mean?" the old man asks his grandson as he leans forward.

The boy takes on a thoughtful expression. After a moment, he tries to put into words what he is thinking and feeling. "It seems that there is always something in history to challenge us…"

The grandfather smiles. "In every generation?"

The boy's face brightens. "Yes, that's it! In every generation someone or something will try to destroy us."

Although the phrase recalled the Passover seder, the grandfather chose to return the discussion to something the children would understand – Purim. And not only Purim but the connection between Purim and Chanukah made by understanding the powerful symbols of the holidays, the dreidle and the groegger.

Both spinning objects… but with very different properties and lessons!

\* \* \*

On Chanukah and Purim, we Jews take pleasure in spinning objects. They needn't be shining or beautiful in and of themselves. Actually, each in its own way, teaches us a valuable lesson of the holiday. And it is not only young people who love to spin the dreidle at Chanukah or spin the *gragger* at Purim.

Spin, spin, spin.

Each object spins but the one teaches us by how it lands and the other drowns out the cruelty of history. There is another significant difference between the two. At Chanukah, when we spin the dreidle, we do so by pinching the stem as it sticks out the top. But during Purim, we grasp the *gragger* from the bottom and then spin it to generate its harsh noise.

Just like a piece of music holds as much beauty in its rests as in the notes played, the difference in these two objects is significant. There are no coincidences in God's world and in the connection between these two objects we learn a very important and profound lesson.

Rabbi Tzvi Elimelech Shapira, author of *B'nei Yissaschar*, explains the difference as follows: God wishes to constantly bestow only abundant blessing upon His nation, but we must initiate with an "inspiration from below." If we create an opening the size of the "eye of a needle," then God, in turn, will respond by "opening up the gateway to a large banquet hall." (Shir HaShirim Rabba, 5:3)

All that God asks is that we take that first step – no matter how modest – toward behaving appropriately in the world and He will answer with such an outpouring of supernatural kindness that we will be astonished and our faith will be upheld and strengthened.

Even a small amount of Torah, repentance, and mitzvot, opens the gates wide, allowing boundless "inspiration from above" to come our way, inspiration which very often takes the form of miracles.

### Purim – bottom up!

In Shushan long ago, in the days of Purim, when their lives hung by a delicate thread, the Jewish People united in sincere prayer and repentance to create an inspiration from below worthy of God's promise to reciprocate. Each individual's sincerity was small, but their *collective* efforts to rescind the harsh decree issued against them were large. They were successful in opening up the gates of heaven for many hidden miracles that brought about their salvation. With the tremendous effort of repentance on the part of the community of the Jewish People, Haman was subsequently destroyed.

So it is that while we listen to the reading of the Scroll of Esther on Purim, we spin the *gragger* from below at the utterance of Haman's name – not only to create the noise that would drown out his name so that it would never be heard but *by the very action we take* to proudly demonstrate that the Jewish people initiated the overwhelming response from the heavens above; as in the world, so in the *grogger* – first the bottom part spins, and only then does its upper part follow in kind.

**Chanukah – top down!**

Unlike Purim, Chanukah teaches us a very different lesson. During the time of Antiochus, our prayer and repentance were not as sincere. The people had assimilated. They were "as the Greeks" and so, in the beginning it was a mere handful of Hasmoneans leading the charge while most of our nation failed to demonstrate the inspiration from below to earn God's abundant blessing from above.

And yet God showered us with miracles. Despite the people's lack of faith, He provided us, mercifully, with inspiration from above. His inspiration was undeserved – which made it all the more miraculous!

And so, the specific miracles arrived and we emerged victorious victors; we re-dedicated the grand Temple and lit a miraculously burning oil.

On Chanukah we spin dreidles upon which are inscribed the first letters of the words, "*neis gadol ha'yah sham*" – a great miracle happened there. (Although it is important to note that, in Israel the letters on the dreidles spell out "*neis gadol ha'yah po*" – a great miracle happened here!) We rejoice with our dreidels, but we spin them specifically from their top part to constantly remind ourselves that Chanukah was a time when miracles came undeserved from God, when the Almighty bestowed His infinite compassion upon His people and things began to spin down to us in the form of undeniable miracles.

**Playing Games**

Of course, the purpose of spinning these two objects is different as well, and this difference also teaches us a great deal about the two holidays. We "play" dreidle by spinning it for *gelt*. Whether the dreidle lands on the "*gimmel*" and the winner takes the whole pot, or the "*shin*" and money is lost – the player is at the mercy of a luck and fate, forces completely outside his control. We watch the dreidle spin and waver, never knowing how long the spinning will last.

The lesson is clear – if we don't take the initial step in triggering God's promise to reciprocate in disproportionate fashion favorable to us, then we leave ourselves up to simply hoping for the best, wishing for God's undeserved mercy.

At Purim time, on the other hand, we spin our noisy *graggers* as partners in the demise of the wicked Haman. The cacophonous sound of the *gragger* teaches us that we had a hand in erasing Haman's evil from the world – just as we have an active role in making sure that his name is forever "drowned out."

Even the raucous sound of the *gragger* teaches us a lesson. The noise – and it *is* noise! – of the *gragger* is not pleasing at all. In and of itself, it does not bring us joy or pleasure. This teaches us that many of the things we do to bring about an important result are not pleasant. Our fasting, our tears and our heartfelt repentance are not always pleasant. But the result is joyous!

We learn that when we accept our responsibility, God assures us that He will fulfill His promise to us. So, on Purim, as opposed to the Chanukah when the dreidle is left to spin, subject to the laws of physics and gravity rather than by us, the *gragger's* spin is completely controlled by us.

There is more to learn from that wobbling, faltering, delightful dreidle than the stem at the top or that it tends to fall according to forces beyond our control. As has been said too many times and in too many places, "Life is like a top. You spin around a lot and then you fall over."

Those who blithely state such things often compare life to a game. And some actually believe that. Life is a game. A joke. An arbitrary happenstance. They wear tee shirts that proclaim, "The One Who Dies With the Most Toys Wins."

No sentiment could be further from the Jewish view. To the Jewish people, life – history – has been anything but a game. Our peoplehood stretches back over 3,000 years. There may be those who think of history as an arbitrary string of barely-related events which too often result in tragedy, providing "evidence" of the futility of life.

But the dreidle bears a very different message.

How surprising that the dreidle, silly top, should carry such weight – not only a theological truth and a statement about the role of the Jewish people in the miracle of Chanukah but also insight and knowledge into powerful historical dynamics. The Kabbalah, the compendium of Jewish mystical teachings, teaches us another aspect of the dreidel. In this understanding, the four letters do not represent a statement about God's presence in the world – a great miracle happened there/here – but rather they each represent one of four different historical empires – Babylonian, Persian, Greek and Roman – that tried to destroy the Jewish people.

Four empires the likes of which the world had never seen. And the Jewish people? A relatively puny gathering of people dedicated to study and the performance of God's command. Is it any wonder that, when given the opportunity, we seek to assimilate and become part of these "great" cultures and empires? But something always holds us back. Internally and externally, we are *different*. We are "like" but not the same.

So, against this backdrop of world history, are we simply spinning haphazardly from one tragedy to another? Or might there be some *reason* and meaning behind all the events that have punctuated our history?

The dreidle teaches us its lesson when we are facing times of hardship and tragedy. And that lesson? It is first and foremost, that God is our God and we are His people. And if we believe in that ultimate meaning of the Jewish people; if we *know* that despite the dizzying blur of events in our history there is some purpose to it all, and if we are prepared *to fight* to remain Jews regardless of what history throws at us, then who knows - we might just see a miracle and be reassured that there is a hidden hand guiding the destiny of the Jewish people.

Isn't that the lesson in our modern state of Israel?

Some sixty years ago, for the first time since the Maccabees defeated the Greeks, the Jewish people were on the verge of reclaiming sovereignty in their homeland. Who in all the world believed that the birth of this new state would happen at all? And even if it should be born, it would quickly be extinguished at the hands of the much larger and far better equipped Arab armies.

In those early days, the Jews of Palestine built up an image of strength for political reasons. They had to convince a doubting world that they were capable of surviving the birth pangs of nationhood. Their image was so persuasive that even the Arabs were fooled.

How different the reality was from the image!

The fledgling Jewish army could barely arm a quarter of its men. It possessed a few thousand rifles, less than a thousand machine guns, and sufficient ammunition for only three days fighting. There were no heavy armaments of any kind – no heavy machine guns, no artillery, no anti-tank or anti-aircraft guns, no real armored cars.

No air force.

No navy.

Then things turned worse. On December 5, 1947, the United States government announced a total embargo on arms sales to the Middle East. By that time, the Arabs had already purchased tens of millions of dollars worth of U.S. arms surplus. The Jews had nothing but their anemic supplies and a dream.

The rest, as they say in another well-worn quote, "is history."

\* \* \*

We Jews are a people of history. God, whose name defines His nature as being outside of time, has entered time to save us, to establish and to reestablish His relationship with us.

That is the true miracle of our lives, that in the thicket of history, we can be lost for so long and then found again.

That is the miracle of the dreidle.

It is our story. It is my story.

It is our history. Told on the sides of a modest, little top.